THE AUSTRALIAN
Women's Weekly

EVERYDAY
GLUTEN FREE

THE AUSTRALIAN WOMEN'S WEEKLY
TRIPLE TESTED
TEST KITCHEN

BAUER MEDIA GROUP

PUBLISHED IN 2017 BY BOUNTY BOOKS BASED ON MATERIALS
LICENSED TO IT BY BAUER MEDIA BOOKS, AUSTRALIA.

BAUER MEDIA BOOKS IS A DIVISION OF
BAUER MEDIA PTY LIMITED,
54 PARK ST, SYDNEY; GPO BOX 4088,
SYDNEY, NSW 2001, AUSTRALIA
PH +61 2 9282 8618; FAX +61 2 9126 3702
WWW.AWWCOOKBOOKS.COM.AU

PUBLISHER
JO RUNCIMAN

EDITORIAL & FOOD DIRECTOR
SOPHIA YOUNG

DIRECTOR OF SALES, MARKETING & RIGHTS
BRIAN CEARNES

EDITORIAL DIRECTOR-AT-LARGE
PAMELA CLARK

CREATIVE DIRECTOR
HANNAH BLACKMORE

DESIGNER
MENG KOACH

MANAGING EDITOR
STEPHANIE KISTNER

JUNIOR EDITOR
AMANDA LEES

FOOD EDITORS
LOUISE PATNIOTIS, ALEXANDRA ELLIOTT

OPERATIONS MANAGER
DAVID SCOTTO

PRINTED IN CHINA
BY LEO PAPER PRODUCTS LTD.

PUBLISHED AND DISTRIBUTED IN THE
UNITED KINGDOM BY BOUNTY BOOKS,
A DIVISION OF OCTOPUS PUBLISHING GROUP LTD
CARMELITE HOUSE
50 VICTORIA EMBANKMENT
LONDON, EC4Y 0DZ
UNITED KINGDOM
INFO@OCTOPUS-PUBLISHING.CO.UK;
WWW.OCTOPUSBOOKS.CO.UK

INTERNATIONAL FOREIGN LANGUAGE RIGHTS
BRIAN CEARNES, BAUER MEDIA BOOKS
BCEARNES@BAUER-MEDIA.COM.AU

A CATALOGUE RECORD FOR THIS BOOK IS
AVAILABLE FROM THE BRITISH LIBRARY.

ISBN: 978-0-7537-3259-5

© BAUER MEDIA PTY LTD 2017
ABN 18 053 273 546

THE AUSTRALIAN
Women's Weekly

EVERYDAY
GLUTEN FREE

THE AUSTRALIAN WOMEN'S WEEKLY

TRIPLE TESTED

TEST KITCHEN

Bounty
Books

CONTENTS

What is GLUTEN?

What is a gluten-free diet and should you be following one?

Gluten is a mixture of proteins found in some grains, principally wheat — including the increasingly popular ancient wheat varieties spelt, Kamut® khorasan wheat, einkorn and emmer — rye, barley and triticale (a cross between wheat and rye).

These grains make good bread principally because of gluten. It absorbs water, gives elasticity to the dough and the end result is a chewier, lighter textured bread. You'll find that gluten-free breads tend to be denser and tougher as a result of not containing gluten. In most people gluten does not cause any problems and is digested alongside all other proteins. However, in a growing number of people, gluten is a problem and gluten-free diets have increased in popularity.

COELIAC DISEASE

Coeliac disease affects an estimated 1 in 70 Australians, although many will be unaware of it, attributing their symptoms to general food intolerances or irritable bowel syndrome. But it's absolutely essential to get a proper diagnosis as there can be serious health consequences without the proper treatment – that is a lifelong, strictly gluten-free diet.

It is absolutely crucial to get a proper diagnosis for coeliac disease. A strictly gluten-free diet is not as easy as it sounds – gluten itself or gluten-containing ingredients are frequently used in food products you might not expect including sauces and condiments, and although most cafes and restaurants have become savvier about catering for special diets, they may not always get it right. Hence you want to know how careful you need to be with avoiding all sources of gluten.

GLUTEN SENSITIVITY

In the absence of coeliac disease it is possible to have an intolerance to

Coeliac disease affects an estimated 1 in 70 Australians, although many will be unaware of it.

gluten. However, this is less easy to diagnose. As with all food intolerances the immune system is not involved and therefore allergy blood tests do not identify the problem food. It can only be done through trial and error, testing, eliminating and re-testing with the suspected foods.

If you are having gut symptoms your doctor should be your first port of call to eliminate any medical cause and rule out or confirm coeliac disease. In the absence of any medical reason for your problems, then seeing an Accredited Practising Dietitian who specialises in food intolerances is your best way of identifying the problem and the most suitable diet for you.

If gluten sensitivity is suspected the good news is that you needn't be strictly gluten free – usually small levels of gluten can be tolerated. This makes the diet much easier to follow than the strictly gluten-free diet for the treatment of coeliac disease.

GLUTEN-CONTAINING *foods*

Wheat
Bulgur, farro, freekeh, spelt, emmer, Kamut®, einkorn, durum wheat, bread, tortillas, wraps, breakfast cereals, granola, croissants, pasta, couscous, noodles, pastries, semolina, farina, pies, doughnuts, biscuits, cake, banana bread, muffins, cupcakes, crumbed meat and fish, and sauces where wheat flour has been used to thicken e.g. béchamel sauce and gravies.

Rye
Bread, pumpernickel bread, wraps, breakfast cereals, rye beer & rye whiskey, crispbreads, crackers.

Barley
Bread, wraps, breakfast cereals, malt extract, beer, whiskey, malt vinegar.

Triticale
Biscuits, crispbreads, cookies, slices, cakes, muffins & bread.

Alcoholic Drinks
Wine and distilled spirits are gluten free, however beers, ales and lagers made from gluten-containing grains (commonly barley) are not gluten free. With the rise in those following gluten-free diets there are now a number of gluten-free beers available in Australia and around the world. These are most commonly made from millet or sorghum and "gluten free" will be clearly indicated on the label.

Packaged Foods
Flour is often used in processing, even when you least expect it. For example, frozen chips may have wheat flour used to aid in creating a crispy coating, or a processed fruit bar may have flour used to help bind the product. If you need to be strictly gluten free, become an expert at reading food labels! There are also a number of Apps that can help you identify gluten-free products, even by simply scanning the barcode.

* Note that wheat-free foods are not necessarily gluten-free and a wheat-free diet is not the same as a gluten-free diet. This is a common confusion. Some people have an intolerance to wheat, but are fine with other gluten-containing grains. This is another reason to ensure that you have a correct diagnosis to ensure you are following the optimal diet for you.

DELICIOUS
MORNINGS

Buckwheat waffles
WITH GOLDEN SYRUP

PREP + COOK TIME 45 MINUTES SERVES 8

- ⅓ cup (60g) dairy-free spread
- 2 tablespoons caster (superfine) sugar
- 3 eggs, separated
- ⅓ cup (45g) gluten-free plain (all-purpose) flour
- ⅓ cup (50g) buckwheat flour
- ⅓ cup (50g) 100% corn (maize) cornflour (cornstarch)
- 1 cup (135g) gluten-free self-raising flour
- 1 teaspoon gluten-free baking powder
- 1 teaspoon bicarbonate of soda (baking soda)
- ½ teaspoon salt
- ½ teaspoon ground cinnamon
- 1½ cups (375ml) soy milk
- 1½ teaspoons white vinegar
- cooking-oil spray
- 250g (8 ounces) strawberries, halved
- ⅔ cup (230g) golden syrup
- 1 tablespoon gluten-free icing (confectioners') sugar

1 Beat dairy-free spread and sugar in a medium bowl with an electric mixer until light and fluffy. Beat in egg yolks one at a time.

2 Beat egg whites in a small bowl with an electric mixer until soft peaks form. Gently fold egg whites into egg-yolk mixture.

3 Fold sifted dry ingredients, soy milk and vinegar into egg mixture until the mix just comes together. (Do not over mix the waffle mixture; it may look slightly curdled at this stage.)

4 Spray a heated waffle iron with oil; pour ½ cup batter over bottom element of waffle iron. Close iron; cook waffle about 3 minutes or until browned both sides and crisp. Transfer waffle to a plate; cover to keep warm.

5 Repeat step 4 to make a total of 8 waffles. Serve waffles with strawberries, drizzled with golden syrup and dusted with icing sugar.

TIPS

If you don't have a waffle iron, you can cook the waffles in a jaffle iron. Waffles can be frozen in an airtight container for up to 3 months; reheat in a moderate oven for about 15 minutes or until warmed through. You can use your favourite dairy-free milk in this recipe.

**NUTRITIONAL
COUNT PER SERVING**
8.3g total fat
3.3g saturated fat
1252kJ (399 cal)
59g carbohydrate
4.8g protein
0.6g fibre

Plus
**DAIRY FREE
NUT FREE**

NUTRITIONAL
COUNT PER SERVING
13.8g total fat
7g saturated fat
1798kJ (430 cal)
65.9g carbohydrate
8.9g protein
5.7g fibre

Plus
YEAST FREE
EGG FREE

Creamy chai spiced
AMARANTH PORRIDGE

PREP + COOK TIME 40 MINUTES SERVES 4

- 1 cup (185g) amaranth
- 1 teaspoon ground cinnamon
- 1 teaspoon ground cardamom
- 1 teaspoon ground ginger
- 3 cups (750ml) water
- 30g (1 ounce) butter
- 2 ripe corella pears (300g), halved lengthways
- 2 tablespoons pure maple syrup
- 1 cup (250ml) almond milk
- ½ cup (140g) Greek-style yoghurt
- 2 tablespoons pure maple syrup, extra

1 Combine amaranth, cinnamon, cardamom, ginger and the water in a medium saucepan. Bring to the boil over high heat. Reduce heat to low; simmer, stirring occasionally, for 30 minutes or until soft.

2 Meanwhile, melt butter in a medium non-stick frying pan over medium-low heat; cook pears, cut-side down, for 10 minutes or until soft. Increase heat to high, add half the maple syrup; cook until pears are browned and glazed.

3 Add almond milk and remaining maple syrup to amaranth mixture; cook, stirring, until heated through.

4 Serve porridge topped with yoghurt and maple pears; drizzled with extra maple syrup.

TIPS

Amaranth is available from health food stores or bulk wholefood stores. Any type of milk can be used in place of almond milk. Porridge is best made just before serving.

Ham, green onion & ZUCCHINI FRITTERS

PREP + COOK TIME 20 MINUTES **SERVES** 4

- 250g (8 ounces) red grape tomatoes
- 1 teaspoon balsamic vinegar
- 1½ tablespoons olive oil
- 1 small zucchini (90g)
- 1 cup (135g) gluten-free self-raising flour
- ¾ cup (180ml) soy milk
- 250g (8 ounces) gluten-free shaved ham, chopped finely
- 2 green onions (scallions), sliced thinly
- 1 large avocado (320g), chopped coarsely

1 Preheat oven to 200°C/400°F.

2 Place tomatoes on an oven tray; drizzle with vinegar and 1 teaspoon of the oil. Season. Roast for 15 minutes or until tomatoes just soften.

3 Grate zucchini. Using a clean tea towel, squeeze excess moisture from zucchini.

4 Sift flour into a large bowl. Gradually add milk, in batches, stirring after each addition. Add ham, green onion and zucchini; stir to combine. Season.

5 Heat remaining oil in a large non-stick frying pan over medium heat. Spoon about ¼ cup of batter into pan; cook for 2½ minutes each side or until golden brown and cooked through. Repeat with remaining batter to make a total of 8 fritters.

6 Serve fritters with avocado and roasted tomatoes. Top with extra sliced green onion, if you like.

TIPS

You can use your favourite dairy-free milk for this recipe or, if you don't have a dairy allergy, use whichever milk you like. Replace the ham with frozen peas or corn for a vegetarian option. You can make these fritters with regular self-raising flour if you don't have a gluten allergy, though you may need to use less milk.

**NUTRITIONAL
COUNT PER SERVING**
20.3g total fat
4g saturated fat
1372kJ (328 cal)
31.5g carbohydrate
3.4g protein
3g fibre

Plus

DAIRY FREE
YEAST FREE
NUT FREE

**NUTRITIONAL
COUNT PER WRAP**
14.7g total fat
3.8g saturated fat
1518kJ (363 cal)
27g carbohydrate
28.6 protein
2.6g fibre

Breakfast WRAPS

PREP + COOK TIME 50 MINUTES **SERVES** 4

- cooking-oil spray
- 4 eggs
- 4 rindless bacon slices (260g)
- 1 tablespoon dairy-free spread
- 150g (4½ ounces) button mushrooms, sliced thinly
- 60g (2 ounces) baby spinach leaves
- 2 tablespoons gluten-free barbecue sauce

GLUTEN-FREE WRAPS

- 2 eggs
- 1 cup (135g) gluten-free self-raising flour
- ⅓ cup (50g) buckwheat flour
- ⅓ cup (45g) gluten-free plain (all-purpose) flour
- ⅓ cup (50g) 100% corn (maize) cornflour (cornstarch)
- 1½ teaspoons salt
- ⅔ cup (160ml) soy milk
- ⅔ cup (160ml) water

1 Make gluten-free wraps.

2 Spray a medium frying pan with oil; cook eggs over medium heat until the whites are firm and the yolks are cooked to your liking. Transfer eggs to a plate; cover to keep warm.

3 Cook bacon in the same pan until crisp; transfer to a plate, cover to keep warm. Melt dairy-free spread in same heated pan; cook mushrooms over medium heat for 5 minutes or until browned.

4 Divide spinach, mushrooms and bacon between 4 wraps (see tips for storing remaining wraps); drizzle with barbecue sauce then top with egg. Season. Roll wraps to serve.

gluten-free wraps Beat eggs in a small bowl with an electric mixer until thick and pale. Add sifted dry ingredients, and the combined milk and water, alternately, stirring until just combined; do not over mix. Heat a flat sandwich press until light indicates it is ready to use; spray with oil. Pour ⅓ cup of mixture in a circle shape onto press; fully close lid and cook for 2 minutes or until golden brown. Transfer to a plate. Repeat to make a total of 8 wraps.

TIPS

You need a sandwich press with two flat elements. If you don't have one, spread ⅓ cup of batter into a circle shape in a heated large frying pan; cook both sides until brown and cooked through. Unfilled wraps can be made a day ahead; store in the fridge in an airtight container, or freeze for up to 3 months. Reheat wraps in a heated frying pan until warmed through. You will need 4 wraps for this recipe; reserve remaining for another use.

Apricot & fig spiced millet
WITH COCONUT WHIP

PREP + COOK TIME 40 MINUTES (+ STANDING & REFRIGERATION) **SERVES** 6

You will need to start this recipe a day ahead.

- 2 x 400ml cans coconut cream
- 1½ cups (300g) millet
- 2 cups (500ml) apple juice
- 2 cups (500ml) water
- 1 teaspoon ground cinnamon
- 1 teaspoon ground ginger
- ⅔ cup (100g) dried apricots, chopped
- ½ cup (100g) dried figs, chopped
- 1 tablespoon pure maple syrup
- 1 teaspoon vanilla extract
- 1½ tablespoons coconut sugar

1 Refrigerate unopened cans of coconut cream overnight.

2 Place millet in a medium bowl with enough cold water to cover; stand overnight. Drain; rinse well.

3 Place millet in a medium saucepan with juice, the water, spices and dried fruit; bring to the boil. Reduce heat to low; simmer, uncovered, for 15 minutes, stirring occasionally, or until millet is soft. Transfer mixture to a heatproof bowl; cover, refrigerate until cold.

4 Without shaking, open chilled cans of coconut cream; spoon the thick cream on the surface into a medium bowl (store remaining coconut cream for another use; see tips). Beat with an electric mixer until thick and creamy. Add maple syrup and vanilla; beat until combined.

5 Spoon millet mixture into six 1½-cup (375ml) glasses. Top with whipped coconut cream and coconut sugar.

TIPS

The millet can be served hot or cold; if it is served warm the coconut whip will melt quickly. You can use the leftover liquid from the coconut cream in smoothies, curries or soups.

Plus
**DAIRY FREE
YEAST FREE
EGG FREE**

**NUTRITIONAL
COUNT PER BAGEL
(BAGEL ONLY)**
21.8g total fat
4.5g saturated fat
1914kJ (458 cal)
54.9g carbohydrate
8.8g protein
0.7g fibre

Poppy seed BAGELS

PREP + COOK TIME 50 MINUTES (+ STANDING) MAKES 10

- 3⅓ cups (450g) gluten-free plain (all-purpose) flour
- ½ cup (75g) potato flour
- ½ cup (90g) white rice flour
- ½ cup (75g) buckwheat flour
- 3 teaspoons (10g) dried yeast
- 2 teaspoons salt
- 2 teaspoons xanthan gum
- 4 eggs
- ¾ cup (180ml) light olive oil
- 1½ cups (375ml) warm milk, plus 1 tablespoon extra
- 2 teaspoons poppy seeds
- 2 teaspoons flaked sea salt

TIPS

The longer you boil the bagels the chewer they become. Store bagels, wrapped in plastic wrap, in the fridge for up to 2 days or freeze for up to 3 months.

1 Combine sifted flours, yeast, salt and gum in a large bowl.

2 Seperate 3 of the eggs; reserve yolks. Place whole egg and egg whites in a large bowl of an electric mixer with oil and milk; beat on medium speed for 3½ minutes. Add the flour mixture, 1 cup at a time, beating until combined and smooth.

3 Turn dough onto a lightly floured surface and knead until smooth. Divide dough into 10 pieces. Roll each piece into a 24cm (9½-inch) long rope. Working with one length of dough at a time, shape into a ring until ends meet, securing ends together with a little water. Place ring on a greased oven tray. Repeat with remaining dough. Cover with oiled plastic wrap; stand in a warm place for 45 minutes.

4 Preheat oven to 200°C/400°F. Grease two oven trays then line with baking paper.

5 Working in batches of four, drop bagels one by one into a large saucepan of boiling water, ensuring they don't touch; boil for 1 minute. Turn bagels over; boil for another minute. Using a slotted spoon, transfer bagels to lined trays. Repeat with remaining bagels.

6 Brush tops of bagels with combined reserved egg yolks and extra milk; sprinkle with poppy seeds and sea salt. Bake for 25 minutes or until golden. Cool on a wire rack.

serving suggestions Serve lightly toasted, topped with smashed avocado, roasted cherry tomatoes, crumbled fetta and fresh oregano leaves, or simply spread with cream cheese or jam.

Basic MORNING MUFFINS

PREP + COOK TIME 35 MINUTES MAKES 6

- 1 cup (135g) gluten-free self-raising flour
- 1 teaspoon ground cinnamon
- 2 tablespoons white chia seeds
- 1 cup (100g) almond meal
- ½ cup (80g) coconut sugar
- 1 cup (250ml) buttermilk
- ¼ cup (60ml) melted coconut oil
- 1 egg, beaten lightly

1 Preheat oven to 190°C/375°F. Line a 6-hole (½-cup/125ml) muffin pan with paper cases.

2 Sift flour and cinnamon into a large bowl; stir in chia seeds, almond meal and coconut sugar. Make a well in the centre. Whisk buttermilk, coconut oil and egg in a large jug. Pour into dry ingredients; stir until just combined. Spoon mixture into paper cases.

3 Bake muffins for 25 minutes or until cooked when a skewer is inserted and comes out clean. Leave muffins in pan for 5 minutes before transferring to a wire rack.

4 ways with
BASIC MUFFINS

MANGO & COCONUT MUFFINS

PREP + COOK TIME 35 MINUTES MAKES 6

You will need 1 small mango (300g) for this recipe.

Make basic morning muffins following the recipe on page 23, adding 1 teaspoon mixed spice and 2 tablespoons shredded coconut to dry ingredients. Spoon mixture into cases; top with slices of fresh mango and 1 tablespoon extra shredded coconut. Bake for 25 minutes or until muffins are cooked when a skewer is inserted and comes out clean. Leave muffins in pan for 5 minutes before transferring to a wire rack.

HAZELNUT & BANANA CHOCOLATE MUFFINS

PREP + COOK TIME 45 MINUTES MAKES 6

Make basic morning muffins following the recipe on page 23, replacing the almond meal with 1 cup (100g) hazelnut meal to dry ingredients, and the coconut oil with 60g (2oz) melted butter. Spoon mixture into cases, top with 1 piece of sliced banana, 50g (1½oz) chopped dark (semi-sweet) chocolate and ¼ cup (35g) chopped skinless hazelnuts. Bake for 30 minutes or until muffins are cooked when a skewer is inserted and comes out clean. Leave muffins in pan for 5 minutes before transferring to a wire rack.

**NUTRITIONAL
COUNT PER MUFFIN**
2.38g total fat
8.5g saturated fat
1697kJ (405 cal)
39.7g carbohydrate
8.2g protein
3.1g fibre

**NUTRITIONAL
COUNT PER MUFFIN**
21.3g total fat
7g saturated fat
1560kJ (373 cal)
37.1g carbohydrate
7.7g protein
3.5g fibre

RASPBERRY JAM & WHITE CHOCOLATE MUFFINS

PREP + COOK TIME 45 MINUTES MAKES 6

Make basic morning muffins following the recipe on page 23, adding 1 teaspoon mixed spice and 50g (1½oz) chopped white chocolate to dry ingredients and replacing the coconut oil with 60g (2oz) melted butter. Spoon mixture into cases; place 1 teaspoon of raspberry jam into the centre of each muffin. Bake for 30 minutes or until muffins are cooked when a skewer is inserted and comes out clean. Leave muffins in pan for 5 minutes before transferring to a wire rack.

BLUEBERRY & ORANGE MUFFINS

PREP + COOK TIME 40 MINUTES MAKES 6

Make basic morning muffins following the recipe on page 23, adding 2 tablespoons finely grated orange rind and 100g (3oz) fresh blueberries to dry ingredients and replacing the coconut oil with 60g (2oz) melted butter. Spoon mixture into cases. Bake for 30 minutes or until muffins are cooked when a skewer is inserted and comes out clean. Leave muffins in pan for 5 minutes before transferring to a wire rack.

**NUTRITIONAL
COUNT PER SERVING**
30.7g total fat
13.9g saturated fat
2173kJ (519 cal)
32.2g carbohydrate
10.2g protein
4.6g fibre

Blushing BANANA BREAD

PREP + COOK TIME 1 HOUR 20 MINUTES **SERVES** 8

You will need 3 overripe sugar bananas (400g) for the amount of mashed banana in this recipe.

- 1¼ cups (170g) gluten-free self-raising flour
- ½ teaspoon ground cinnamon
- 2 tablespoons sunflower seeds
- 2 tablespoons pepitas (pumpkin seed kernels)
- 2 cups (240g) almond meal
- ¼ cup (40g) coconut sugar
- 2 eggs, beaten lightly
- 180g (5½ ounces) butter, melted, cooled
- 1 cup (260g) mashed overripe banana (see tips)
- 1 small carrot (70g), grated finely
- 1 small beetroot (beet) (100g), grated finely
- 1 teaspoon pepitas (pumpkin seed kernels), extra

1 Preheat oven to 180°C/350°C. Grease an 11cm x 25cm (4½-inch x 10-inch) loaf pan; line base and two long sides with baking paper, extending the paper 5cm (2 inches) over the sides.

2 Sift flour and cinnamon into a large bowl. Stir in seeds, almond meal, coconut sugar, egg, butter and banana. Add carrot and beetroot; fold through mixture until just marbled. Spoon mixture into pan; sprinkle with extra pepitas.

3 Bake bread for 1 hour 10 minutes or until a skewer comes out clean when inserted in the centre. Turn onto a wire rack. Serve warm or cooled.

serving suggestions Serve slices spread with ricotta, butter, cream cheese or dairy-free cream cheese.

TIPS

You can substitute carrot and beetroot with zucchini and pumpkin. It's important the bananas are overripe for this recipe, as they add sweetness to the loaf. For a dairy-free version, use a dairy-substitute spread instead of the butter. The loaf is best made on day of serving. It will keep for up to 3 days in an airtight container, but would be best toasted or warmed after the first day. The loaf can also be sliced and frozen for up to 3 months.

Smashed minty peas
WITH GOAT'S CHEESE & EGGS

PREP + COOK TIME 30 MINUTES SERVES 4

- 4 gluten-free wraps (260g) (see tips)
- 30g (1 ounce) butter
- 4 green onions (scallions), chopped finely
- 500g (1 pound) frozen peas, thawed
- ¼ cup fresh mint leaves, shredded finely
- ⅓ cup (80ml) gluten-free chicken stock
- 4 eggs
- 150g (4½ ounces) drained marinated goat's cheese, crumbled

1 Heat a medium non-stick frying pan over high heat; cook wraps, one at a time, for 30 seconds each side or until heated through. Cover with foil to keep warm.

2 Melt butter in same pan over medium heat; cook green onion, stirring, for 5 minutes or until soft and golden.

3 Add peas, mint and stock; bring to the boil. Reduce heat; simmer, uncovered, for 3 minutes or until peas are soft and bright green. Place half the pea mixture into a heatproof bowl; coarsely mash. Stir through remaining pea mixture; cover to keep warm.

4 To poach eggs, half-fill a large deep frying pan with water, add a pinch of salt; bring to a gentle simmer. Break 1 egg into a cup, then slide into pan. When all eggs are in pan; return to the boil. Cover pan; remove from heat. Stand for 3 minutes or until a light film of egg white sets over the yolks. Remove eggs from pan with a slotted spoon; drain on paper towel.

5 Serve wraps topped with smashed peas, egg and cheese. Season to taste.

TIPS

Use your favourite gluten-free wrap, or make the gluten-free wraps recipe on page 17. The pea mixture can be made ahead of time and then reheated just before serving. Any leftover pea mixture can be added to frittatas or sprinkled over salads.

Plus
YEAST FREE
NUT FREE

NUTRITIONAL
COUNT PER SERVING
24.4g total fat
11.9g saturated fat
2287kJ (546 cal)
52.7g carbohydrate
24.4g protein
9.8g fibre

NUTRITIONAL COUNT PER SERVING
32.7g total fat
10.8g saturated fat
1656kJ (396 cal)
7g carbohydrate
15.8g protein
7.5g fibre

Grilled mushrooms with
DUKKAH EGGS & CRISP KALE

PREP + COOK TIME 25 MINUTES **SERVES 4**

- 4 field mushrooms (400g)
- 1 clove garlic, chopped finely
- 50g (1½ ounces) butter, at room temperature
- 1 tablespoon chopped fresh chives
- ½ cup (50g) walnuts, chopped coarsely
- 4 eggs
- ¼ cup (30g) pistachio dukkah
- 145g (4½ ounces) kale leaves, stalks removed
- 1 tablespoon olive oil
- ⅓ cup (95g) Greek-style yoghurt

1 Preheat the grill (broiler) to high. Line an oven tray with baking paper.

2 Remove and discard stalks from mushrooms; place mushrooms on tray. Combine garlic, butter, chives and walnuts in a small bowl. Spoon butter mixture into centre of each mushroom; cook mushrooms under the grill for 5 minutes or until mushrooms are golden brown and soft, and the nuts are toasted.

3 Meanwhile, cook eggs in a medium saucepan of boiling water for 5 minutes or until soft-boiled; drain. When cool enough to handle, peel eggs; roll in dukkah.

4 Brush kale leaves with oil; cook under grill for 5 minutes or until crisp.

5 Serve mushrooms with eggs, kale and yoghurt.

TIPS

Bring the eggs to room temperature before cooking, that way you can be sure they will be soft cooked.

Coconut almond bread with
PASSIONFRUIT CHIA JAM

PREP + COOK TIME 1 HOUR (+ STANDING & COOLING) **SERVES** 8 (MAKES 1 LOAF)

- ½ cup (65g) gluten-free self-raising flour
- ½ cup (80g) coconut flour
- 1 teaspoon bicarbonate soda (baking soda)
- 1 teaspoon ground cinnamon
- ⅔ cup (150g) caster (superfine) sugar
- ¼ cup (40g) white chia seeds
- ¼ cup (30g) almond meal
- 5 eggs
- ½ cup (125ml) coconut oil, melted
- 1 teaspoon apple cider vinegar
- 1 teaspoon vanilla extract
- ¼ cup (60ml) water
- 2 tablespoons shredded coconut
- 150g (4½ ounces) fresh ricotta
- 2 tablespoons caster (superfine) sugar

PASSIONFRUIT CHIA JAM

- 1 cup (250ml) fresh passionfruit pulp
- 2 tablespoons white chia seeds

1 Make passionfruit chia jam.

2 Meanwhile, preheat oven to 180°C/350°F. Grease a 13cm x 26cm (5¼-inch x 10½-inch) loaf pan (top measurement); line base with baking paper.

3 Sift flours, bicarbonate of soda and cinnamon into a medium bowl; stir in sugar, chia seeds and almond meal. Make a well in the centre.

4 Whisk eggs, coconut oil, vinegar, vanilla and the water in a medium jug. Pour egg mixture into dry ingredients; fold through to form a smooth thick batter. Pour batter into pan; press shredded coconut on top.

5 Bake for 35 minutes or until a skewer inserted in the centre comes out clean. Cool loaf in pan.

6 Combine ricotta and sugar in a small bowl.

7 Serve bread sliced fresh or toasted with ricotta mixture and passionfruit chia jam.

passionfruit chia jam Combine ingredients in a small bowl. Stand for 1 hour or until thick and jam like.

TIPS

You can use fresh or frozen berries to make the jam instead of the passionfruit pulp. Any leftover jam can be stored in an airtight container in the refrigerator for up to 1 week, it will thicken on standing. To make this recipe dairy free replace the ricotta with Tofutti, a tofu-based cream cheese.

Plus
YEAST FREE

Plus
**YEAST FREE
NUT FREE**

Polenta pancake with
PROSCIUTTO & TOMATO

PREP + COOK TIME 1 HOUR SERVES 6

- 2 cups (270g) gluten-free plain (all-purpose) flour
- 2 teaspoons gluten-free baking powder
- ½ cup (85g) fine polenta (cornmeal)
- 150g (4½ ounces) butter, melted, cooled
- 2 cups (500ml) milk
- 4 eggs
- ½ cup (40g) finely grated parmesan
- 30g (1 ounce) butter, extra
- 12 thin slices gluten-free prosciutto (150g)
- 130g (4 ounces) truss cherry tomatoes
- 30g (1 ounce) baby rocket (arugula)
- 1 small avocado (200g), chopped
- 1 medium lemon (140g), cut into wedges

1 Preheat oven to 200°C/400°F. Line an oven tray with baking paper.

2 Sift flour and baking powder into a large bowl; stir in polenta. Make a well in the centre. Whisk butter, milk, eggs and half the parmesan in a jug. Gradually whisk into dry ingredients until batter is smooth.

3 Melt extra butter over base and sides of a 26cm (10-inch) non-stick ovenproof frying pan over medium heat. Pour batter into pan; top with prosciutto. Sprinkle with remaining parmesan; cook for 10 minutes or until edges are set, taking care not to burn the base.

4 Transfer pan to oven; bake for 25 minutes. Top with tomatoes, bake for a further 10 minutes or until pancake is crisp and golden and a skewer inserted in the centre comes out clean.

5 Top polenta pancake with baby rocket and avocado. Serve with lemon wedges. Season to taste.

TIPS

This dish is best served straight from the pan it is cooked in, make sure you grease the pan well to make removing it easier.

Chorizo SHAKSHUKA

PREP + COOK TIME 50 MINUTES **SERVES** 6

- 1 tablespoon olive oil
- 1 medium red onion (170g), chopped finely
- 2 gluten-free cured chorizo sausages (220g), sliced
- 1 teaspoon smoked paprika
- 800g (1½ pounds) canned chopped tomatoes
- 340g (11-ounce) jar fire-roasted pepper strips, drained
- 6 eggs
- 2 tablespoons chopped fresh coriander (cilantro)
- 6 slices gluten-free bread (150g), toasted

1 Heat oil in a 30cm (12-inch) (top measurement) frying pan over medium heat; cook onion, stirring, for 10 minutes or until soft and golden.

2 Add chorizo and paprika; cook, stirring for 5 minutes or until chorizo is browned.

3 Stir in tomatoes and peppers; bring to the boil. Reduce heat to low; simmer, for 20 minutes or until sauce has thickened. Season to taste.

4 Use a large spoon to make six indentations in the sauce; break one egg into each hole. Cook over medium heat for 10 minutes or until eggs are cooked to your liking.

5 Sprinkle shakshuka with coriander. Serve with toast.

TIPS

The sauce can be made ahead of time and then reheated in the morning. You can cook the shakshuka in the oven on 180°C/350°F for 15 minutes, if you like.

**NUTRITIONAL
COUNT PER SERVING**
16.7g total fat
4.6g saturated fat
1319kJ (315 cal)
21.9g carbohydrate
17.2g protein
4.2g fibre

Plus
**NUT FREE
YEAST FREE
EGG FREE**

**NUTRITIONAL
COUNT PER SERVING**
12.3g total fat
7.3g saturated fat
1453kJ (347 cal)
38.1g carbohydrate
16.6g protein
6.1g fibre

Black beans & cheddar
CORN QUESADILLAS

PREP + COOK TIME 25 MINUTES SERVES 4

- 400g (12½ ounces) canned black beans, drained, rinsed
- 1½ teaspoons smoked paprika
- 1 cup (120g) coarsely grated cheddar
- 2 green onions (scallions), sliced thinly
- 8 x 15cm (6-inch) fresh gluten-free white corn tortillas

TIPS

White corn tortilla are available in supermarkets or in health food stores, you could substitute gluten-free yellow corn tortillas, if you like.

1 Combine beans and paprika in a medium bowl; using the back of a fork, coarsely mash. Add cheddar and green onion; mix well, season.

2 Place four of the tortillas on a clean chopping board. Spoon bean mixture evenly over tortillas. Top with remaining tortillas.

3 Heat a medium frying pan over medium heat; cook one quesadilla at a time, pressing down firmly with a spatula, for 5 minutes or until the tortilla is crisp and golden brown. Turn over; cook for a further 3 minutes or until cheddar has melted and tortilla is crisp. Remove from heat, cover with foil to keep warm. Repeat with remaining quesadillas.

4 Cut warm quesadillas in halves and wedges to serve. Accompany with lime wedges and micro coriander leaves, if you like.

Basic coconut PANCAKES

PREP + COOK TIME 30 MINUTES SERVES 4 (MAKES 12 PANCAKES)

You will need 5 small overripe bananas (600g) for the mashed banana in this recipe.

- 1½ cups (360g) mashed banana
- 8 eggs
- 2 teaspoons finely grated lemon rind
- ½ cup (75g) coconut flour
- 1½ tablespoons coconut oil

1 Blend or process mashed banana, eggs, lemon rind and flour until smooth.

2 Heat a little of the coconut oil in a large non-stick frying pan over medium heat; cook ¼ cup of batter for 1 minute or until bubbles appear on the surface. Turn pancakes; cook for 1 minute or until golden. Remove from the pan; cover with foil to keep warm. Repeat with remaining coconut oil and batter to make 12 pancakes in total.

3 Serve with grilled bacon, strawberries and maple syrup, if you like.

serving suggestion Serve pancakes following one of the recipes on pages 42 and 43, if you like.

NUTRITIONAL
COUNT PER SERVING
(PANCAKE ONLY)
20.5 total fat
10.5g saturated fat
1600kJ (382 cal)
21.4g carbohydrate
25.3g protein
4g fibre

4 ways with
COCONUT PANCAKES

Plus
**YEAST FREE
DAIRY FREE**

Plus
**YEAST FREE
DAIRY FREE
NUT FREE**

BLUEBERRY, LEMON & COCONUT PANCAKES

PREP + COOK TIME 30 MINUTES **SERVES** 4

Make pancake batter following basic coconut pancake recipe on page 41. Transfer mixture to a jug, stir in 100g (3oz) blueberries. Heat a little of 1 tablespoon of coconut oil in a large non-stick frying pan over medium heat; cook ¼ cup measures of batter for 1 minute or until bubbles appear on the surface. Turn pancakes; cook for 1 minute or until golden. Remove from pan; cover with foil to keep warm. Repeat with remaining coconut oil and batter to make 12 pancakes in total. Serve each pancake drizzled with 1 teaspoon lemon juice and sprinkled with 1 teaspoon of coconut sugar and extra blueberries, if you like.

BANANA, HONEY & MACADAMIA PANCAKES

PREP + COOK TIME 30 MINUTES **SERVES** 4

Make pancake batter following basic coconut pancake recipe on page 41. Transfer mixture to a jug, stir in ⅔ cup (80g) chopped roasted macadamias. Heat a little of 1 tablespoon of coconut oil in a large non-stick frying pan over medium heat; cook ¼ cup measures of batter for 1 minute or until bubbles appear on the surface. Turn pancakes; cook for 1 minute or until golden. Remove from the pan; cover with foil to keep warm. Repeat with remaining coconut oil and batter to make 12 pancakes in total. Divide slices of 1 medium pan-fried banana, 2 tablespoons honey and ⅓ cup (35g) chopped roasted macadamias between pancake stacks to serve.

**NUTRITIONAL
COUNT PER SERVING**
21.8g total fat
11.2g saturated fat
1884kJ (450 cal)
30.4g carbohydrate
27.8g protein
7.8g fibre

Plus
YEAST FREE
DAIRY FREE
NUT FREE

Plus
YEAST FREE
NUT FREE

**NUTRITIONAL
COUNT PER SERVING**
24.2g total fat
12.7g saturated fat
2187kJ (522 cal)
43g carbohydrate
29.6g protein
5.8g fibre

PANCAKES WITH MANGO, RICOTTA & LIME

PREP + COOK TIME 30 MINUTES **SERVES** 4

Make pancake batter following basic coconut pancake recipe on page 41. Transfer mixture to a jug, stir in 100g (3oz) blueberries. Heat a little of 1 tablespoon of coconut oil in a large non-stick frying pan over medium heat; cook ¼ cup measures of batter for 1 minute or until bubbles appear on the surface. Turn pancakes; cook for 1 minute or until golden. Remove from pan; cover with foil to keep warm. Repeat with remaining coconut oil and batter to make 12 pancakes in total. Combine 125g (8oz) fresh ricotta with 2 teaspoons finely grated lime rind in a small bowl. Serve pancakes topped with ricotta mixture and 2 sliced fresh mangoes and a good squeeze of lime juice. Drizzle with 2 tablespoons of pure maple syrup.

PANCAKES WITH BERRIES & COCONUT YOGHURT

PREP + COOK TIME 30 MINUTES **SERVES** 4

Make pancake batter following basic coconut pancake recipe on page 41. Heat a little of 1 tablespoon of coconut oil in a large non-stick frying pan over medium heat; cook ¼ cup measures of batter for 1 minute or until bubbles appear on the surface. Turn pancakes; cook for 1 minute or until golden. Remove from pan; cover with foil to keep warm. Repeat with remaining batter to make 12 pancakes in total. Serve pancakes topped with ⅓ cup (95g) coconut yoghurt and 100g (3oz) fresh mixed berries.

Plus
**EGG FREE
NUT FREE**

**NUTRITIONAL
COUNT PER CRUMPET**
1g total fat
0.2g saturated fat
404kJ (97 cal)
20g carbohydrate
1g protein
0.5g fibre

Crumpets with
RHUBARB COMPOTE

PREP + COOK TIME 1 HOUR (+ STANDING) MAKES 16

You need 4 egg rings for this recipe.

- 2 teaspoons (7g) dry yeast
- 1½ cups (375ml) warm water
- 1½ cups (200g) gluten-free plain (all-purpose) flour
- ½ cup (75g) 100% corn (maize) cornflour (cornstarch)
- 1½ teaspoons salt
- 2 tablespoons brown sugar
- ¼ cup (60ml) soy milk
- 1 tablespoon dairy-free spread
- ⅓ cup (95g) Greek-style yoghurt or coconut yoghurt
- 1 tablespoon gluten-free icing (confectioners') sugar

RHUBARB COMPOTE

- 300g (9½ ounces) trimmed rhubarb, cut into 4cm (1½-inch) lengths
- 1 cinnamon stick
- 1 tablespoon finely grated orange rind
- 1¼ cups (310ml) freshly squeezed orange juice
- ¼ cup (55g) caster (superfine) sugar

TIPS

You can use your favourite dairy-free milk for this recipe or, if you don't have a dairy allergy, use whichever milk you like. Crumpets are best made just before serving.

1 Combine yeast and ¼ cup of the warm water in a small bowl. Cover; stand in a warm place for 10 minutes or until mixture is frothy.

2 Sift flours into a medium bowl; stir in salt and sugar. Make a well in the centre. Gradually whisk in milk and the remaining warm water until combined. Add yeast mixture; whisk until smooth. Cover; stand in a warm place for 30 minutes or until mixture has risen slightly.

3 Melt dairy-free spread.

4 Heat a large heavy-based frying pan over low heat. Brush a little of the melted spread over base of pan and around the insides of four 2cm (¾-inch) deep egg rings; place rings in pan.

5 Pour 2 tablespoons of the batter into each ring; cook, uncovered, until bubbles appear and the surface is a little dry. Using an egg slide, turn rings; cook for 1 minute or until crumpets are cooked through. Remove from pan; cover to keep warm. Repeat to make 16 crumpets in total, brushing pan and rings with melted spread between each batch.

6 Meanwhile, make rhubarb compote.

7 Serve crumpets topped with compote and yoghurt; dusted with icing sugar.

rhubarb compote Combine ingredients in a medium saucepan over medium heat; simmer, covered, for 5 minutes or until rhubarb is tender. (Makes 2 cups)

Salted carob LATTE

PREP + COOK TIME 10 MINUTES SERVES 2 (MAKES 3 CUPS)

- 1 vanilla bean
- 3 cups (750ml) soy milk
- 1½ tablespoons carob powder
- pinch of salt flakes
- 1 tablespoon raw honey
- ¼ teaspoon carob powder, extra

TIPS

Carob powder is a natural, caffeine-free alternative to cocoa powder. It is available from health food stores and online. Use your favourite milk in this recipe.

1 Split a vanilla bean lengthways, scrape seeds from one pod half using the tip of a knife; add seeds and pod half to a small saucepan. Reserve the remaining pod half for another use. Add milk, carob powder, salt and honey to pan. Place pan over low-medium heat; simmer, stirring continuously, for 5 minutes or until carob powder dissolves and mixture is heated.

2 Discard pod. Transfer to a blender; blend until frothy. Pour into heatproof glasses; dust with extra carob powder.

Plus
**NUT FREE
DAIRY FREE
EGG FREE**

**NUTRITIONAL
COUNT PER SERVING**
11.3g total fat
1.9g saturated fat
1174kJ (281 cal)
33.7g carbohydrate
7.9g protein
3.1g fibre

Plus
EGG FREE NUT FREE

NUTRITIONAL COUNT PER SERVING
7.6g total fat
4.6g saturated fat
731kJ (175 cal)
20.5g carbohydrate
7.4g protein
2.4g fibre

Warm golden TURMERIC MILK

PREP + COOK TIME 10 MINUTES   SERVES 4 (MAKES 3¾ CUPS)

Turmeric has been use in traditional Indian and Chinese medicine for centuries for its anti-inflammatory, anti-oxidant and anti-cancer properties.

- 2 tablespoons grated fresh red turmeric
- 3 cups (750ml) full cream milk or nut or plant milk of your choice
- ½ teaspoon ground turmeric
- 1 teaspoon ground cinnamon
- pinch black pepper
- 1 tablespoon coconut sugar

1 Stir fresh turmeric, milk and dried spices in a medium saucepan over medium heat for 10 minutes or until milk is heated and just about to boil.

2 Remove pan from heat; stir in coconut sugar.

TIPS

Golden milk is best made ahead of time and left to stand, this way the flavour and the colour infuse into the milk. Any leftover milk can be stored in an airtight container in the refrigerator. You can use honey instead of sugar, if you like.

Hot smoked salmon with
HERBED SCRAMBLED EGGS

PREP + COOK TIME 30 MINUTES **SERVES** 4

- 8 eggs
- 2 tablespoons chopped fresh chives
- 2 tablespoons chopped fresh dill
- 20g (¾ ounce) butter
- 10g (½ ounce) butter, extra
- ⅓ cup (65g) capers, drained, pat dry (see tips)
- 4 slices gluten-free bread (150g), toasted
- 300g (9½ ounces) hot smoked salmon, flaked
- dill sprigs, to serve

1 Whisk eggs, chives and dill in a medium jug; season.

2 Melt butter in a medium non-stick frying pan over medium heat. Add egg mixture; cook, without stirring for 1 minute or until egg starts to set, then use a wide spatula to gently scrape the set egg mixture along the base of the pan; cook until creamy and barely set. Remove pan from heat.

3 Melt extra butter in a small frying pan over high heat; cook capers, stirring, for 3 minutes or until crisp.

4 Serve scrambled egg with toast, topped with salmon, capers and dill springs.

TIPS

The capers need to be fairly dry for them to go crisp when they are fried so make sure you drain them well on the paper towel first.

Plus
YEAST FREE
NUT FREE

**NUTRITIONAL
COUNT PER SERVING**
6.4g total fat
1.3g saturated fat
516kJ (123 cal)
13.2g carbohydrate
2.3g protein
3.5g fibre

Green SMOOTHIE

PREP + COOK TIME 10 MINUTES **SERVES** 4 (MAKES 1 LITRE)

- 1 small celery stalk (55g), chopped
- 2 cups (90g) chopped kale leaves
- 2 cups (500ml) chilled coconut water
- 1 small ripe pear (180g), cored, chopped
- 1 medium ripe banana (200g), sliced
- ½ medium ripe avocado (125g), sliced
- 1 tablespoon finely grated fresh ginger
- 1 tablespoon white chia seeds
- 1 cup ice cubes

1 Place celery, kale, and coconut water into a high-powered blender; blend until smooth.

2 Add pear, banana, avocado, ginger, chia seeds and ice; blend until smooth and creamy.

TIPS

Green smoothies have a basic formula which is roughly 2 cups greens, 2 cups liquid and 2 cups fruit. Experiment with your fruit combinations using whatever is in season. Serve with sliced pear and sprinkled with chia seeds, if you like.

Overnight buckwheat,
ALMOND & ORANGE PORRIDGE

PREP + COOK TIME 15 MINUTES (+ STANDING) **SERVES** 4

You will need to start this recipe a day ahead.

- 1 cup (200g) buckwheat
- 1 cup (160g) natural almonds
- 2 small red apples (260g), unpeeled, grated coarsely
- 2 teaspoons finely grated orange rind
- 1 cup (250ml) freshly squeezed orange juice
- 1 tablespoon nut butter
- 1 teaspoon orange blossom water
- 2 teaspoons raw honey
- 1 medium orange (240g), segmented
- ¼ cup (40g) pomegranate seeds
- 50g (1½ ounces) blueberries
- 2 tablespoons pepitas (pumpkin seed kernels)
- 2 tablespoons raw honey, extra

1 Place buckwheat and almonds into 2 separate bowls; cover with cold water, stand overnight. Drain, rinse; drain well.

2 Transfer buckwheat and almonds to a food processor or blender. Add apple, rind, juice, nut butter, orange blossom water and honey; process until smooth and creamy, scraping down the sides of the blender, as necessary.

3 Serve buckwheat porridge topped with orange segments, pomegranate seeds, blueberries and pepitas. Drizzle with extra honey.

TIPS

You can use any nut in place of the almonds but remember that soaked almonds are one of the most digestible of all the nuts.

**NUTRITIONAL
COUNT PER SERVING**
5.7g total fat
3.4g saturated fat
1003kJ (340 cal)
38.2g carbohydrate
4.3g protein
9.6g fibre

Acai fruit bowl topped with
CHIA, COCONUT & FRUIT

PREP + COOK TIME 25 MINUTES SERVES 4

*You will need to start this recipe a day ahead
to freeze the banana.*

- ½ cup (125ml) chilled water
- 2 frozen chopped bananas (250g)
- 1 cup (200g) chopped red papaya
- 1 tablespoon acai powder (see tips)
- 200g (6½ ounces) frozen raspberries
- 1 medium banana (200g), sliced
- 100g (3 ounces) dragon fruit, sliced
- 1 small mango (300g), sliced
- 2 kiwifruit (170g), sliced
- 1 teaspoon black chia seeds
- ½ cup (25g) flaked coconut, toasted

1 Place the water, frozen bananas, papaya, acai powder and
raspberries in a high-powered blender; blend until smooth.
2 Divide mixture between serving bowls; top with remaining
ingredients. Serve immediately.

TIPS

Acai berry powder is available at chemists.
You can vary the fruit and the toppings you
use for this recipe depending on what is
in season. Try topping your acai bowl with
some gluten-free granola, such as the
puffed grain maple granola on page 59.

Raspberry sago with
COCONUT YOGHURT

PREP + COOK TIME 30 MINUTES (+ STANDING & COOLING) **SERVES** 4

- 1 litre (4 cups) water
- 1 cup (200g) pearl sago or seed tapioca
- 200g (6½ ounces) frozen raspberries, thawed, crushed coarsely
- 200g (6½ ounces) coconut yoghurt
- 2 tablespoons chopped pistachios
- 100g (3 ounces) raspberries, extra

1 Bring the water to the boil in a medium saucepan. Add sago; cook, stirring occasionally, for 10 minutes or until sago is soft and translucent.

2 Transfer sago to a heatproof bowl; stir in raspberries. Cool completely.

3 Spoon sago into four serving glasses or jars; top with coconut yoghurt, pistachios and extra raspberries.

TIPS

This recipe has no sugar added as often coconut yoghurt is sweetened. Taste it and see how much sweetness the raspberries add as sometimes these can be a little sour. Use pure maple syrup to sweeten.

Plus
**DAIRY FREE
YEAST FREE
EGG FREE**

**NUTRITIONAL
COUNT PER SERVING**
3.1g total fat
0.4g saturated fat
919kJ (220 cal)
44.9g carbohydrate
1.4g protein
2.2g fibre

**NUTRITIONAL
COUNT PER CUP**
36.9g total fat
15.5g saturated fat
2152kJ (514 cal)
30.3g carbohydrate
13.6g protein
6.2g fibre

Puffed grain maple
GRANOLA

PREP + COOK TIME 35 MINUTES (+ COOLING) **MAKES** ABOUT 11 CUPS

- 2 cups (45g) puffed corn
- 2 cups (90g) puffed amaranth
- 4 cups (100g) puffed quinoa
- 2 teaspoons ground cinnamon
- 1 cup (75g) shredded coconut
- 1 cup (150g) sunflower seeds
- 1 cup (200g) pepitas (pumpkin seed kernels)
- ⅔ cup (110g) raw almonds
- ½ cup (125ml) coconut oil, melted
- ¼ cup (60ml) pure maple syrup
- ⅔ cup (100g) dried apricot halves, chopped
- ⅓ cup (30g) dried goji berries

1 Preheat oven to 180°C/350°F. Line two large baking trays with baking paper.

2 Combine puffed corn, amaranth and quinoa in a large bowl with cinnamon, coconut, seeds and almonds.

3 Combine coconut oil and maple syrup in a small jug; pour over dry ingredients. Stir well to combine. Spread granola mixture onto trays.

4 Bake for 25 minutes or until crisp and golden, stirring occasionally. Cool on trays. Place cooled granola in a large bowl; stir in apricots and goji berries.

serving suggestion Serve granola with your favourite yoghurt and fresh fruit.

TIPS

Granola can be stored in an airtight container for up to 3 weeks.

Vanilla roasted hazelnut
& CACAO SMOOTHIE

PREP + COOK TIME 5 MINUTES **SERVES** 2 (MAKES 3 CUPS)

- ½ cup (70g) roasted skinned hazelnuts
- 1 teaspoon vanilla bean paste
- 1 small ripe sugar banana (130g), sliced
- 1 tablespoon cacao powder
- 2 cups (500ml) chilled almond milk
- 1 tablespoon pure maple syrup
- 1 cup ice cubes
- ½ teaspoon cacao powder, extra

1 Place hazelnuts, vanilla paste, banana, cacao powder, almond milk and syrup in a high-powered blender; blend until smooth and creamy.

2 Pour smoothie over ice. Serve dusted with extra cacao.

TIPS

This is a very protein dense smoothie with a large amount of nuts, you could reduce the amount of hazelnuts and add 1 tablespoon of chia seeds, if you prefer.

Chia & buckwheat
GRANOLA POTS

PREP + COOK TIME 1½ **HOURS** (+ **COOLING, STANDING & REFRIGERATION**) **SERVES** 4

You will need to start this recipe a day ahead.

- ¾ cup (150g) buckwheat
- ¼ cup (40g) raw cashews
- ¼ cup (35g) sunflower seeds
- ¼ cup (40g) pepitas (pumpkin seed kernels)
- ⅓ cup (80ml) apple juice
- ¼ cup (30g) dried goji berries
- 400ml can coconut cream
- 1 teaspoon vanilla extract
- 1 tablespoon honey
- ¼ cup (40g) white chia seeds
- 250g (8 ounces) strawberries, sliced
- 60g (2 ounces) blueberries

1 Combine buckwheat, cashews and seeds in a medium bowl; add enough cold water to cover. Stand overnight. Drain well. Add apple juice. Stand for 1 hour.

2 Preheat oven to 180°C/350°F. Line an oven tray with baking paper.

3 Spread buckwheat mixture on tray. Bake for 25 minutes or until golden and dry, stirring occasionally. Transfer to a heatproof bowl; stir in goji berries. Cool completely.

4 Meanwhile, combine coconut cream, vanilla, honey and chia seeds in a medium bowl. Cover; refrigerate for 1 hour or until it forms a soft gel.

5 Spoon granola mixture into base of serving glasses. Top with chia mixture then strawberries and blueberries.

TIPS

The buckwheat granola mixture is delicious eaten as a stand alone meal; store any leftover in an airtight container. It is also delicious served on top of yoghurt.

LUNCH
ON THE GO

Spinach & fetta BREAD ROLLS

PREP + COOK TIME 1 HOUR (+ STANDING) **MAKES** 8

- 1 bunch spinach (280g)
- 3 cups (405g) gluten-free plain (all-purpose) flour
- ½ cup (75g) potato flour
- ½ cup (80g) brown rice flour
- ½ cup (80g) white rice flour
- 3 teaspoons (10g) dried yeast
- 2 teaspoons salt
- 2 teaspoons xanthan gum
- 1 egg
- 3 egg whites
- ¾ cup (180ml) olive oil
- 1 teaspoon vinegar
- 2 cups (500ml) warm water
- 200g (6½ ounces) crumbled fetta

1 Grease and line an oven tray with baking paper.

2 Wash and trim spinach; place in a heatproof bowl. Pour boiling water over spinach; stand for 1 minute. Drain. Rinse under cold water; drain. Squeeze excess water from spinach. Roughly chop.

3 Combine sifted flours, yeast, salt and gum in a large bowl.

4 Place egg, egg whites, oil, vinegar and 1½ cups of the warm water in a large bowl of an electric mixer; beat on medium speed for 3½ minutes. Add remaining water and the flour mixture, 1 cup at a time, beating until mixture is combined and smooth. Fold chopped spinach and fetta through dough.

5 Divide dough into eight portions. With wet hands, roll portions into balls. Place on oven tray. Cover; stand in a warm place for 45 minutes.

6 Preheat oven to 220°C/425°F.

7 Bake rolls for 40 minutes or until golden in colour and rolls sound hollow when tapped. Leave rolls on tray for 5 minutes before transferring to a wire rack to cool. Serve warm.

TIPS

These rolls are best eaten on the day they are made. Freeze for up to 3 months. Microwave cold rolls in 10-second bursts until heated through. Serve rolls with slices of cheddar, if you like.

**NUTRITIONAL
COUNT PER ROLL**
28.0g total fat
7.1g saturated fat
2354kJ (562 cal)
61.0g carbohydrate
14.6g protein
3.4g fibre

Plus
**NUT FREE
YEAST FREE
EGG FREE**

**NUTRITIONAL
COUNT PER ROLL**
33.9g total fat
15.9g saturated fat
2393kJ (572 cal)
52.1g carbohydrate
13.1g protein
1.3g fibre

Sausage ROLLS

PREP + COOK TIME 1 HOUR 10 MINUTES (+ REFRIGERATION) **MAKES** 6

- 2 teaspoons olive oil
- 1 small leek (200g), chopped finely
- 1 small carrot (70g), grated finely
- 1 clove garlic, crushed
- 300g (9½ ounces) gluten-free sausage mince
- ½ teaspoon gluten-free roast lamb seasoning
- 1 tablespoon tomato paste
- 3 teaspoons sesame seeds or poppy seeds

GLUTEN-FREE PASTRY
- 2¾ cups (375g) gluten-free pastry flour
- 125g (4 ounces) cold butter, chopped coarsely
- ⅔ cup (160ml) water
- 2 tablespoons tamari
- 2 tablespoons olive oil
- gluten-free plain (all-purpose) flour, for dusting

1 Make gluten-free pastry.

2 Heat oil in a medium frying pan over high heat; cook leek, carrot and garlic, stirring, for 5 minutes or until soft. Cool.

3 Combine mince, seasoning, paste and vegetable mixture in a medium bowl; season.

4 Roll the pastry between sheets of baking paper until 4mm (¼-inch) thick; cut into six 12cm (6½-inch) squares. Spoon ⅓ cup of mixture down one edge of each square. Roll to enclose. Brush edges with a little water; press to seal. Score pastry with a sharp knife; sprinkle with seeds. Refrigerate for 30 minutes or until firm.

5 Preheat oven to 180°C/350°F. Grease and line an oven tray with baking paper. Place rolls on tray.

6 Bake rolls for 20 minutes or until pastry is browned lightly and filling is cooked through. Serve with gluten-free tomato sauce (ketchup), if you like.

gluten-free pastry Place pastry flour in a large bowl; rub in butter until mixture resembles coarse breadcrumbs. Add enough of the combined water, tamari and oil until mixture comes together. Lightly knead on a surface dusted with a little gluten-free flour into a ball.

TIPS

Pastry is best used straight away. If pastry dries out while you are using it, add a little olive oil to the dough. You can use store-bought gluten-free puff pastry, available from major supermarkets.

69

Lamb & ROSEMARY PIES

PREP + COOK TIME 2½ HOURS (+ COOLING & REFRIGERATION) **MAKES** 6

- 1 tablespoon olive oil
- 800g (1½ pounds) boneless lamb shoulder, cut into 2cm (¾-inch) pieces
- 2 medium brown onions (300g), chopped finely
- 1 clove garlic, crushed
- 2 sprigs fresh rosemary
- 2 tablespoons tomato paste
- 1 tablespoon dijon mustard
- 2½ cups (625ml) gluten-free chicken stock
- 2 tablespoons 100% corn (maize) cornflour (cornstarch)
- 2 tablespoons water
- 1 cup (120g) frozen peas, thawed

GLUTEN-FREE PASTRY
- 2¾ cups (375g) gluten-free pastry flour
- 125g (4 ounces) cold butter, chopped coarsely
- ⅔ cup (160ml) water
- 2 tablespoons tamari
- 2 tablespoons olive oil
- gluten-free plain (all-purpose) flour, for dusting

TIPS

You can use store-bought gluten-free puff pastry, available from major supermarkets. The pies can be cooked in an electric pie maker. Freeze pies for up to 3 months; reheat from frozen in a 180°C/350°F oven for 30 minutes or until pies are heated through.

1 Heat oil in a medium saucepan over high heat; cook lamb, in batches, stirring, for 2 minutes or until browned. Remove from pan.

2 Reduce heat to medium; cook onion and garlic in same pan, stirring, for 5 minutes or until onion is softened. Return lamb to pan with rosemary and combined paste, mustard and chicken stock; bring to the boil. Reduce heat to low; simmer, uncovered, stirring occasionally, for 1½ hours or until lamb is tender and sauce thickens.

3 Combine cornflour and the water; add to lamb mixture with peas; cook, stirring, over high heat, for 5 minutes or until sauce boils and thickens. Season, cool.

4 Meanwhile, make gluten-free pastry.

5 Preheat oven to 220°C/425°F. Oil six 10cm (4-inch), ¾ cup (180ml) pie dishes. Place dishes on an oven tray.

6 Roll pastry between two sheets of baking paper until 4mm (¼ inch) thick. Cut six 15cm (6-inch) rounds from pastry. Ease pastry rounds into dishes; press into base and sides, trim edges.

7 Spoon lamb mixture into pastry cases. Brush edges with water. Cut six 10cm (4-inch) rounds from remaining pastry; place on pies, press to seal, trim edges. Refrigerate for 30 minutes.

8 Make two small cuts into the top of each pie. Bake pies for 30 minutes or until tops are firm, browned lightly and filling is hot. Serve with steamed green beans and gluten-free oven-baked chips, if you like.

gluten-free pastry Place pastry flour in a large bowl; rub in butter until mixture resembles coarse breadcrumbs. Add enough of the combined water, tamari and oil until mixture comes together. Lightly knead on a surface dusted with a little gluten-free flour into a ball.

**NUTRITIONAL
COUNT PER PIE**
34.8g total fat
16.3g saturated fat
2897kJ (692 cal)
60.3g carbohydrate
31.8g protein
2.9g fibre

**NUTRITIONAL
COUNT PER SERVING**
26.8g total fat
10.7g saturated fat
2484kJ (593 cal)
51.1g carbohydrate
33.9g protein
6.4g fibre

Zucchini & QUINOA SLICE

PREP + COOK TIME 1 HOUR (+ COOLING) SERVES 4

- 1½ cups (300g) quinoa
- 1½ cups (375ml) water
- 2 teaspoons olive oil
- 3 rindless bacon slices (195g), chopped coarsely
- 1 medium brown onion (150g), chopped finely
- 2 medium zucchini (240g), grated coarsely
- 5 eggs, beaten lightly
- 1 cup (100g) coarsely grated tasty cheese
- 1½ tablespoons french mustard

TIPS

This slice can be cooked the day before and packed into lunch boxes for school or work. Store covered in the fridge.

1 Preheat oven to 180°C/350°F. Grease a 20cm x 30cm (8-inch x 12-inch) rectangular slice pan; line base and long sides with baking paper, extending the paper 5cm (2 inches) over the sides.

2 Rinse quinoa under cold running water until water runs clear; drain well. Place quinoa in a medium saucepan with the water over high heat; bring to the boil. Reduce heat to low; cook, covered, for 15 minutes or until liquid is absorbed. Cool.

3 Meanwhile, heat oil in a medium non-stick frying pan, over medium heat; cook bacon and onion, stirring, for 5 minutes or until onion is soft.

4 Place quinoa and bacon mixture in a large bowl, add remaining ingredients; stir until combined. Pour mixture into pan; smooth the surface.

5 Bake slice for 40 minutes or until browned and firm to touch. Cool in pan. Cut slice into 8 squares, then cut each square into triangles. Serve topped with micro herbs, if you like.

serving suggestion Serve with chilli sauce and a mixed leaf salad.

Goat's cheese & fig jam
ROAST BEEF ON FLATBREAD

PREP + COOK TIME 1½ HOURS **SERVES** 4 (MAKES 10 FLATBREADS)

- 650g (1¼-pound) blade beef roast
- 1 teaspoon cracked black pepper
- 1 clove garlic, crushed
- 1 tablespoon finely grated lemon rind
- 2 tablespoons extra virgin olive oil
- 1 medium lemon (140g)
- 150g (4½-ounce) tub fig and walnut paste
- 50g (1½ ounces) baby rocket (arugula) leaves
- 100g (3 ounces) soft goat's cheese

FLATBREAD

- 1½ cups (225g) buckwheat flour
- 1½ cups (225g) 100% corn (maize) cornflour (cornstarch)
- 2 eggs, beaten lightly
- 2 tablespoons extra virgin olive oil
- ¾ cup (180ml) water, approximately

1 Preheat oven to 180°C/350°F.

2 Coat beef in combined pepper, garlic, rind and half the oil. Season. Place in an oiled baking tray. Roast beef for 50 minutes or until cooked as desired. Cover tightly with foil; rest for 10 minutes before slicing.

3 Meanwhile, make flatbread.

4 Remove rind from lemon with a zester. (Or, peel rind thinly from lemon avoiding white pith. Cut rind into long thin strips.)

5 To serve, spread four flatbread with paste, top with beef, rocket, and crumbled cheese. Drizzle with remaining oil, sprinkle with strips of lemon rind. Season. Top with micro herbs, if you like.

flatbread Combine flours in a medium bowl; make a well in the centre. Add egg, half the oil and enough water to form a soft dough. Knead on a floured surface until smooth. Divide dough into 10 portions; roll each portion into a 3mm (⅛-inch) thick, 20cm (8-inch) oval. Brush flatbread with remaining oil; cook on a heated grill pan (or barbecue) for 3 minutes each side or until browned and crisp.

TIPS

Wrap remaining flatbreads in plastic wrap and freeze for up to 3 months. These are also great to use as pizza bases.

NUTRITIONAL
COUNT PER SERVING
38g total fat
13g saturated fat
4492kJ (1073 cal)
111g carbohydrate
66.6g protein
1.5g fibre

Plus
**DAIRY FREE
YEAST FREE
EGG FREE**

Pumpkin, ginger & CASHEW PATTIES

PREP + COOK TIME 50 MINUTES (+ REFRIGERATION) SERVES 4

You will need to start this recipe a day ahead.

- 400ml can coconut cream
- 900g (1¾ pounds) pumpkin, peeled, chopped
- 2 teaspoons ground turmeric
- 2 teaspoons ground cumin
- 2 teaspoons black mustard seeds
- ⅓ cup (50g) sunflower seeds
- ½ cup (75g) coarsely chopped roasted cashews
- 1 cup (40g) finely shredded kale
- 2 teaspoons finely grated fresh ginger
- 2 tablespoons black chia seeds
- ⅔ cup (100g) coconut flour
- ⅓ cup (80g) coconut oil
- ¼ cup (70g) drained pickled ginger
- 150g (4½ ounces) mixed salad leaves

1 Refrigerate unopened can of coconut cream overnight.

2 Boil, steam or microwave pumpkin until soft; drain. Place pumpkin in a large heatproof bowl; mash. Cool slightly.

3 Heat a medium frying pan over medium heat; dry-fry spices for 1 minute or until fragrant.

4 Add spices, sunflower seeds, cashews, kale, fresh ginger, chia seeds, half the coconut flour and a pinch of salt to pumpkin; mix well to combine. Shape mixture into eight patties (the patties will be soft). Carefully coat patties in remaining coconut flour; place on a baking-paper-lined tray. Refrigerate patties for 15 minutes.

5 Heat coconut oil in a large non-stick frying pan over medium heat; cook patties, for 5 minutes each side or until golden brown and cooked through. Drain on paper towel.

6 To make the coconut cream, open chilled can of coconut cream; spoon the thick cream on the surface into a small bowl of an electric mixer (store remaining cream for another use; see tips). Beat coconut cream with electric beater until thick and creamy.

7 Serve patties topped with coconut cream and pickled ginger, and with salad leaves.

TIPS

The uncooked patties can be made ahead of time, sorted covered in the refrigerator. Patties can be served hot or cold. Sweet potato can be substituted for the pumpkin. Any leftover whipped coconut cream can be served with fresh fruit or as a dairy-free replacement for cream.

Chicken, olive &
FETTA SALAD

PREP + COOK TIME 40 MINUTES **SERVES** 4

- 500g (1 pound) chicken breast fillets
- 1 medium lemon (140g), sliced
- ½ cup (60g) frozen peas
- 3 green onions (scallions)
- 1 medium green cucumber (170g)
- 1 baby cos (romaine) lettuce (180g)
- 1 cup (50g) firmly packed alfalfa sprouts
- ¼ cup fresh mint leaves
- ⅔ cups (100g) pitted kalamata olives
- 150g (4½ ounces) danish fetta, crumbled

MUSTARD DRESSING

- 1 tablespoon verjuice
- 1½ tablespoons wholegrain mustard
- ½ teaspoon pure maple syrup
- 2 tablespoons extra virgin olive oil

1 Place chicken in a medium saucepan with enough cold water to cover. Add lemon slices; bring to a simmer. Simmer over low heat, for 20 minutes or until chicken is tender. Transfer chicken to a plate, discard poaching liquid. Cool; shred chicken.

2 Make mustard dressing.

3 Place peas in a small heatproof bowl, cover with boiling water; stand 1 minute or until peas are bright green. Drain. Refresh under cold water; drain.

4 On a large board, chop green onions, cucumber, lettuce, sprouts and mint, gathering mixture together until combined. Place mixture in a large bowl; stir in chicken, peas, olives and fetta.

5 Serve drizzled with mustard dressing. Season to taste.

mustard dressing Place ingredients in a screw-top jar; shake well. Season.

TIPS

Mustard dressing can be made up to a week ahead; store in a jar in the fridge. Salad is best made just before serving.

Plus

NUT FREE
YEAST FREE
EGG FREE

NUTRITIONAL COUNT PER SERVING
28.9g total fat
8g saturated fat
1779kJ (425 cal)
6.2g carbohydrate
33.7g protein
2.8g fibre

NUTRITIONAL
COUNT PER SERVING
24.5g total fat
9.4g saturated fat
2775kJ (663 cal)
67.5g carbohydrate
34.2g protein
20.2g fibre

Plus
NUT FREE
YEAST FREE
EGG FREE

Curried lentil
COTTAGE PIE

PREP + COOK TIME 1 HOUR 25 MINUTES **SERVES** 4

- 1 cup (200g) French-style green lentils
- 2 tablespoons olive oil
- 1 large red onion (300g), chopped finely
- 2 cloves garlic, chopped
- 2 teaspoons curry powder
- 1 teaspoon black mustard seeds
- 1 teaspoon ground cinnamon
- 1 medium carrot (120g), chopped
- 1 stalk celery (150g), trimmed, chopped
- 1 medium red capsicum (bell pepper) (200g), chopped
- 2 medium zucchini (240g), sliced
- 200g (6½ ounces) cauliflower, cut into florets
- 800g (1½ pounds) canned chopped tomatoes
- 1 cup (250ml) water
- 2 tablespoons currants
- 800g (1½ pounds) orange sweet potato, chopped coarsely
- ½ cup (40g) grated parmesan
- 1 cup (125g) coarsely grated gruyère cheese

1 Place lentils in a medium saucepan of boiling water; boil, uncovered, for 10 minutes or until just tender (do not overcook or they will be mushy). Drain.

2 Heat oil in a large saucepan; cook onion, stirring, over a medium heat for 10 minutes or until soft and golden. Add garlic and spices; cook, stirring, for 1 minute or until fragrant. Add carrot, celery, capsicum, zucchini, cauliflower, tomatoes, the water and currants; bring to the boil. Reduce heat; simmer, covered, for 30 minutes or until sauce thickens. Stir in lentils.

3 Meanwhile, boil, steam and microwave sweet potato until soft; drain. Mash sweet potato until smooth; swirl through half the combined cheeses.

4 Preheat oven to 200°C/400°F.

5 Spoon lentil mixture into a 20cm x 30cm (8-inch x 12-inch) oval ovenproof dish. Top with sweet potato mash, sprinkle with remaining combined cheeses. Bake pie for 20 minutes or until golden brown and bubbling.

TIPS

Don't overcook lentils in step 1 as they will continue to cook when baked.

Brown rice &
VEGETABLE FRITTATA

PREP + COOK TIME 50 MINUTES SERVES 6

- 8 eggs
- 3 green onions (scallions), chopped
- ½ cup (50g) finely grated parmesan
- ¼ cup (40g) brown rice flour
- ½ cup (85g) cooked long-grain brown rice (see tips)
- 100g (3 ounces) roasted red capsicum (bell pepper), drained, sliced
- 1 cup (125g) coarsely grated jap pumpkin
- 25g (¾ ounce) baby spinach leaves
- 2 tablespoons shredded fresh basil leaves
- 1 tablespoon baby basil leaves

1 Preheat oven to 180°C/350°F. Grease a 23cm (9-inch) square cake pan; line base and sides with baking paper.

2 Lightly whisk eggs in a large bowl. Add green onion, half the parmesan and the flour; whisk to combine. Season well.

3 Pour egg mixture into pan; sprinkle over rice. Arrange capsicum, pumpkin, spinach and shredded basil on top. Sprinkle with remaining parmesan.

4 Bake frittata for 35 minutes or until the egg is set and top is golden. Serve topped with baby basil leaves.

TIPS

This is a great recipe for using leftover rice, otherwise you will need to cook about 2 tablespoons of uncooked rice. You could use pre-packaged microwave rice to save time. Roasted red capsicum is available from delis or bottled in supermarkets. Frittata can be served warm or cooled, ideal for a picnic.

**NUTRITIONAL
COUNT PER SERVING**
25.8g total fat
5.6g saturated fat
2095kJ (500 cal)
46.7g carbohydrate
17.7g protein
8.3g fibre

Beetroot & lentil fritters
WITH CANDIED WALNUTS

PREP + COOK TIME 50 MINUTES SERVES 4 (MAKES 24 FRITTERS)

You will need about 450g (14½ ounces) trimmed beetroot (beets) for the amount of grated beetroot in this recipe.

- ½ cup (100g) French-style green lentils
- 4 cups (400g) coarsely grated beetroot (beets)
- 100g (3 ounces) ricotta
- 3 green onions (scallions), chopped
- 2 tablespoons chopped fresh chives
- ½ cup (75g) buckwheat flour
- 2 eggs, beaten lightly
- 1 teaspoon finely grated lemon rind
- olive oil, for shallow-frying
- ⅓ cup (95g) Greek-style yoghurt
- 30g (1 ounce) baby rocket (arugula)

CANDIED WALNUTS

- 1½ tablespoons brown sugar
- 1 tablespoon pure maple syrup
- 1 tablespoon water
- ½ cup (50g) walnuts

1 Make candied walnuts.

2 Add lentils to a medium saucepan of boiling water; boil, uncovered, for 10 minutes or until tender. Drain. You will need 1¼ cups (250g) cooked lentils.

3 Combine lentils, beetroot, ricotta, green onion, chives, flour, egg and rind in a large bowl. Season.

4 Heat enough oil in a large frying pan to come 2cm (¾-inch) up the side of the pan; cook heaped tablespoons of beetroot mixture in batches, over medium heat, for 2 minutes each side or until golden and cooked through. Drain on paper towel; cover to keep warm.

5 Serve fritters with yoghurt and rocket, and topped candied walnuts.

candied walnuts Preheat oven to 180°C/350°F. Line an oven tray with baking paper. Place sugar, syrup and the water in a small saucepan; stir over medium heat, without boiling, until sugar dissolves. Bring to the boil; boil, uncovered, without stirring, for 5 minutes until mixture is thick and sticky. Remove pan from heat; quickly stir in nuts. Pour mixture onto tray. Bake for 5 minutes or until golden; cool.

TIPS

You can use 1¼ cups rinsed and drained canned lentils if you prefer. Candied walnuts can be made up to 1 day ahead. Store in an airtight container in a cool dry place.

Salmon kale tacos with
QUINOA & PICKLED VEGETABLES

PREP + COOK TIME 45 MINUTES (+ COOLING) **SERVES** 4

- 1 medium carrot (120g), cut into ribbons
- 1 lebanese cucumber (130g), cut into ribbons
- 3 trimmed radish (45g), sliced thinly
- ½ cup (125ml) rice wine vinegar
- 1 tablespoon coconut sugar
- 1 cup (250ml) water
- ½ cup (100g) white quinoa, rinsed
- 1 cup (250ml) water
- 2 tablespoons chopped fresh coriander (cilantro) leaves
- 2 tablespoons lime juice
- 1 tablespoon tamari
- ½ teaspoon sesame oil
- 4 large kale leaves (180g), stalks removed
- 300g (9½ ounces) smoked salmon
- 1 small avocado (200g), quartered, sliced
- ½ teaspoon toasted sesame seeds

1 Preheat oven to 180°C/350°F. Line two large oven trays with baking paper.

2 Place carrot, cucumber and radish into a medium glass bowl.

3 Combine vinegar, coconut sugar and the water in a small saucepan over low heat; stir until sugar dissolves. Bring to the boil; simmer, uncovered, for 5 minutes. Pour over vegetables in bowl; cool.

4 Rinse quinoa under cold running water until liquid runs clear; drain well. Place quinoa in a medium saucepan with the water; bring to the boil. Reduce heat to low; cook, covered, for 15 minutes or until liquid is absorbed. Rinse under cold water; drain well. Place quinoa in a medium bowl; stir in coriander, juice, tamari and oil. Season.

5 Meanwhile, remove stalks from kale, keeping leaves intact; season. Place on trays. Roast kale for 5 minutes or until warm and slightly crisp around the edges.

6 Arrange kale leaves on serving plates to form "taco shells". Top kale with quinoa, smoked salmon, avocado and pickled vegetables; sprinkle with sesame seeds.

TIPS

The quinoa mixture and pickled vegetables can be made a day ahead. The leftover pickled vegetables can be stored in a glass jar in the refrigerator for up to 2 weeks. They make a great addition to salads, stir-fries or wraps.

Plus
NUT FREE
DAIRY FREE
EGG FREE

Plus

**DAIRY FREE
YEAST FREE
EGG FREE**

**NUTRITIONAL
COUNT PER SERVING**
59.7g total fat
9.6g saturated fat
3175kJ (759 cal)
34g carbohydrate
18.2g protein
11.8g fibre

Rainbow salad bowls
WITH SEEDED AVOCADO

PREP + COOK TIME 35 MINUTES (+ STANDING & COOLING) **SERVES** 4

You will need to start this recipe a day ahead.

- 3 cups (750ml) water
- ½ cup (100g) brown teff grains (see tips)
- 2 medium carrots (240g)
- 170g (5½ ounces) asparagus, cut into 5cm (2-inch) pieces
- 250g (8 ounces) beetroot (beets), peeled, grated coarsely
- 2 medium avocados (500g), halved, scooped
- 100g (3 ounces) mixed salad leaves
- 100g (3 ounces) mixed salad sprouts
- ½ cup (80g) tamari almonds, chopped
- 1 tablespoon black sesame seeds
- 1 tablespoon white sesame seeds
- ½ teaspoon sea salt
- 2 tablespoons lemon juice
- 2 tablespoons extra virgin olive oil

CASHEW CREAM

- ⅔ cup (100g) raw cashews
- ½ teaspoon ground turmeric
- 1 tablespoon dijon mustard
- 1 tablespoon extra virgin olive oil
- ½ teaspoon honey
- ¼ cup (60ml) water

1 Make cashew cream.

2 Bring the water to the boil in a medium saucepan; add teff and a pinch of sea salt. Cook, covered, for 10 minutes or until soft. Drain; rinse under cold water. Drain well. Transfer to a medium bowl; cool. Fold half the cashew cream through teff; season.

3 Prepare carrots with a spiralizer, or cut into long thin strips. Pour boiling water over asparagus in a medium heatproof bowl; stand 1 minute, drain. Refresh under cold water; drain.

4 Divide teff mixture between four shallow bowls. Top with beetroot, carrot, asparagus, avocado and salad leaves; sprinkle with sprouts and almonds.

5 Heat a small frying pan over medium heat; dry-fry seeds and salt, for 30 seconds or until they begin to pop. Using a mortar and pestle lightly pound seed mixture to break open some of the seeds.

6 Sprinkle seed mixture over avocado. Drizzle salad bowls with combined juice and oil. Serve bowls with remaining cashew cream.

cashew cream Place cashews in a medium bowl; cover with water. Stand overnight. Drain cashews. Process cashews with turmeric, mustard, oil, honey and the water until smooth and creamy. Season to taste.

TIPS

Teff is a small African grain with a mild flavour, available from health food stores. If unavailable, you can substitute white quinoa. Rinse quinoa thoroughly and cook it for 10 minutes in simmering water or until tender; drain. Cashew cream can be made 2 days ahead.

Herbed falafel with
MILLET TABBOULEH

PREP + COOK TIME 1 HOUR (+ STANDING & REFRIGERATION) **SERVES** 4

You will need to start this recipe a day ahead.

- 1¼ cups (250g) dried chickpeas (garbanzo beans)
- ½ cup (100g) millet
- 1 clove garlic, peeled, quartered
- 1 teaspoon ground cumin
- ¼ cup loosely packed fresh coriander (cilantro) leaves
- ¼ cup loosely packed fresh flat-leaf parsley leaves
- 1 tablespoon olive oil
- 200g (6½ ounces) cherry tomatoes, quartered
- 3 green onions (scallions), chopped
- 1 cup chopped fresh mint leaves
- 1 cup chopped fresh flat-leaf parsley leaves
- ¼ cup (60ml) olive oil
- 2 tablespoons lemon juice
- 1 medium green cucumber (170g), cut into strips
- vegetable oil, for shallow-frying
- mint leaves, extra

TAHINI CREAM
- 2 tablespoons hulled tahini, at room temperature
- 2 tablespoons lemon juice
- 2 tablespoons Greek-style yoghurt
- 2 tablespoons water, approximately

1 Place chickpeas in a large bowl; cover with water, stand overnight. Drain; rinse well. Place millet into a small bowl; cover with water, stand overnight.

2 To make falafel, process chickpeas with garlic, cumin, coriander, parsley and oil until finely chopped and holding together. Season. Process to combine.

3 Press tablespoons of falafel mixture into balls; place on a baking-paper-lined oven tray. Refrigerate for 30 minutes.

4 Meanwhile, drain millet; rinse and drain well. Cook millet in a medium saucepan of boiling water, uncovered, for 10 minutes or until soft; drain. Rinse millet under cold water; drain well.

5 Place millet, tomato, green onion, mint and chopped parsley, olive oil and juice in a large bowl; toss well. Season to taste.

6 Make tahini cream.

7 Heat enough oil in a large frying pan to come 2cm (¾-inch) up the side of the pan; cook falafel in batches, over medium heat, for 3 minutes each side or until crisp and golden. Drain on paper towel; cover to keep warm.

8 Serve falafel with tahini cream, millet tabbouleh and cucumber; sprinkle with extra mint.

tahini cream Whisk tahini, juice and yoghurt in a small bowl; whisk in enough of the water to reach a pouring consistency. Season to taste.

TIPS

The chickpea mixture needs to be very finely chopped, so pulse it several times, then push the mixture down the side of the food processor bowl to ensure the mixture sticks together. The best way to keep falafel warm and crisp is to place them, uncovered, on a wire rack over an oven tray in the oven at 120°C/250°F. Falafel and tahini cream can be prepared a day ahead. Keep both covered, separately, in the refrigerator. Serve with char-grilled gluten-free tortillas or wraps, if you like.

NUTRITIONAL COUNT PER SERVING
49.1g total fat
7.1g saturated fat
2916kJ (697 cal)
29.4g carbohydrate
27.2g protein
21g fibre

Plus
**NUT FREE
YEAST FREE
EGG FREE**

NUTRITIONAL COUNT PER SERVING
53.1g total fat
24.4g saturated fat
3480kJ (831 cal)
38.5g carbohydrate
48.3g protein
4.5g fibre

Plus
**YEAST FREE
NUT FREE**

Spinach buckwheat crêpes
WITH CHICKEN & AVOCADO

PREP + COOK TIME 50 MINUTES (+ STANDING) SERVES 4

- 1 cup (150g) buckwheat flour
- 2 eggs
- ½ cup (125ml) coconut milk
- ½ cup (125ml) gluten-free oat milk
- ½ cup (125ml) water
- 1 tablespoon coconut oil, melted
- ½ teaspoon ground turmeric
- 30g (1 ounce) baby spinach leaves
- 2 tablespoons olive oil
- 50g (1½ ounces) mixed salad leaves
- 2 small avocados (400g), sliced
- 100g (3 ounces) snow pea sprouts, trimmed

CHICKEN BASIL FILLING

- 3 cups (480g) shredded cooked chicken
- ½ cup (120g) sour cream
- 1 tablespoon dijon mustard
- ¼ cup shredded fresh basil leaves
- ¼ cup finely chopped fresh dill
- 1 tablespoon lime juice

1 Process flour, eggs, milks, the water, coconut oil, turmeric and spinach until smooth. Season; pulse until combined. Transfer to a medium bowl; stand for 30 minutes or until thickened slightly.

2 Heat 1 teaspoon at a time of the oil in a 26cm (10½-inch) (top measurement) non-stick frying pan over medium heat. Pour ⅓ cup of the crêpe mixture into pan, swirling around to form a thin crêpe; cook for 1 minute each side or until golden brown. Remove from pan; cover to keep warm. Repeat with remaining oil and batter to make 8 crêpes in total.

3 Make chicken basil filling.

4 Divide salad leaves, avocado, sprouts and filling between crêpes; roll up to enclose. Cut in half to serve.

chicken basil filling Combine ingredients in a medium bowl. Season to taste.

TIPS

You will need 1 large barbecued chicken (900g/1¾-pounds) for the amount of shredded chicken needed. You can use your favourite milk in this recipe. Crêpes can be made a day ahead; microwave each crêpe for 10 seconds before filling. Crêpes can be layered with pieces of baking paper and frozen in an airtight container for up to 3 months.

Pumpkin & cauliflower soup
WITH TAHINI CREAM

PREP + COOK TIME 1 HOUR 45 MINUTES (+ STANDING) **SERVES** 4

- 750g (1½ pounds) jap pumpkin, skin on (see tips)
- 500g (1 pound) parsnips, cut into rounds
- ¼ cup (60ml) olive oil
- 500g (1 pound) cauliflower, broken into small florets
- 1 teaspoon cumin seeds
- 1 large brown onion (200g), chopped
- 1 litre (4 cups) gluten-free chicken stock
- ¼ cup (40g) pomegranate seeds
- ¼ cup loosely packed fresh flat-leaf parsley

TAHINI CREAM
- 2 tablespoons hulled tahini, at room temperature
- ¼ cup (70g) Greek-style plain yoghurt
- 1 tablespoon lemon juice
- 1 teaspoon water (optional)

TIPS

Roasting pumpkin in one large piece with the skin on gives you a much sweeter soup. Soup and tahini cream can be made a day ahead. Cauliflower is best roasted close to serving.

1 Preheat oven to 200°C/400°F. Line two oven trays with baking paper.

2 Place pumpkin and parsnip on one tray; drizzle with 1 tablespoon of the oil. Season. Place cauliflower on remaining tray, drizzle with 1 tablespoon of the oil and sprinkle with cumin seeds; season. Roast parsnip and pumpkin for 45 minutes or until soft. Remove parsnip when it is tender (it may cook faster than the pumpkin). Roast cauliflower for 40 minutes or until golden and slightly charred.

3 Scoop the flesh from the pumpkin; discard skin.

4 Heat remaining oil in a large saucepan over medium heat; cook onion for 10 minutes or until soft and golden. Add pumpkin flesh, parsnip and stock; bring to the boil. Reduce heat; simmer, covered, for 15 minutes. Stand for 10 minutes to cool slightly.

5 Blend or process soup, in batches, until smooth. Return soup to same pan over low heat; stir until hot. Season.

6 Meanwhile, make tahini cream.

7 Serve soup with a dollop of tahini cream, cauliflower, pomegranate and parsley. Season.

tahini cream Combine tahini, yoghurt and juice in a medium bowl. Thin down with the water, if necessary. Season to taste.

Plus
**NUT FREE
YEAST FREE
EGG FREE**

**NUTRITIONAL
COUNT PER SERVING**
22.1g total fat
3.6g saturated fat
1845kJ (441 cal)
40.3g carbohydrate
12.5g protein
16.3g fibre

**NUTRITIONAL
COUNT PER SERVING**
11.1g total fat
1.8g saturated fat
1368kJ (327 cal)
26.5g carbohydrate
22.1g protein
17g fibre

Rice noodle soup with
TOFU & VEGETABLES

PREP + COOK TIME 45 MINUTES **SERVES** 4

- 2 tablespoons tamari
- 1 teaspoon coconut sugar
- ½ teaspoon sesame oil
- 300g (8 ounces) hard tofu, cut into 2cm (¾-inch) slices lengthways
- 1.75 litres (7 cups) gluten-free chicken stock
- 2 star anise
- 1 cinnamon stick
- 1 medium brown onion (150g), cut into thin wedges
- 4 black peppercorns
- 1 bulb garlic, halved
- 4cm (1½-inch) piece fresh ginger (20g), sliced thinly
- ⅓ cup (20g) dried sliced shiitake mushrooms
- 100g (3 ounces) thick dried rice noodles
- 200g (6½ ounces) broccolini, cut into florets
- 125g (4 ounces) baby corn, halved lengthways
- 1 cup (150g) shelled edamame
- 100g (3 ounces) snow peas, trimmed
- 450g (14½ ounces) baby buk choy

1 Combine tamari, sugar and oil in a small shallow bowl. Add tofu; turn to coat.

2 Place stock, star anise, cinnamon, onion, peppercorns, garlic, ginger and mushrooms in a large saucepan. Bring to the boil over medium heat. Reduce heat to medium-low; simmer, covered, for 35 minutes. Discard star anise, cinnamon, peppercorns and garlic.

3 Meanwhile, preheat grill (broiler). Line an oven tray with foil; grease foil. Remove tofu from marinade; reserve marinade. Place tofu on tray; place under grill for 3 minutes each side or until browned on both sides. Cover to keep warm.

4 Place noodles in a large heatproof bowl, cover with boiling water and reserved marinade; stand for 5 minutes or until just softened. Drain; rinse well.

5 Add vegetables to stock mixture; simmer, covered, for 5 minutes or until vegetables are just tender. Season to taste.

6 Divide noodles between four bowls; ladle stock and vegetables over; top with tofu.

TIPS

This is a richly-flavoured stock. You can substitute thinly sliced beef or chicken for the tofu. Recipe is best made close to serving. Serve soup drizzled with chilli oil, if you like.

Roast vegetable tart
WITH PUMPKIN TAHINI CREAM

PREP + COOK TIME 1½ HOURS (+ REFRIGERATION) **SERVES** 4

- 1 medium red capsicum (bell pepper) (200g), sliced thickly
- 1 large red onion (300g), sliced into thin wedges
- 2 large zucchini (300g), sliced
- 2 medium carrots (240g), quartered lengthways, halved
- 500g (1 pound) jap pumpkin, unpeeled, cut into thick wedges
- 200g (6½ ounces) cauliflower, cut into small florets
- 2 tablespoons olive oil
- 2 tablespoons unhulled tahini, at room temperature
- 1 small clove garlic, crushed
- 2 tablespoons lemon juice
- 1 tablespoon pomegranate molasses
- 1 teaspoon sesame seeds, toasted
- 1 tablespoon micro basil, optional

SESAME PASTRY
- 2 cups (300g) chickpea (besan) flour
- ½ cup (80g) brown rice flour
- ⅓ cup (50g) sesame seeds
- 2 teaspoons sea salt flakes
- ⅓ cup (80ml) olive oil
- ½ cup (125ml) water

1 Preheat oven 200°C/400°F. Line two large oven trays with baking paper.

2 Place vegetables on oven trays; drizzle with oil and season. Roast for 45 minutes or until vegetables are tender and slightly charred. Reduce oven to 180°C/350°F.

3 Make sesame pastry.

4 Grease two large oven trays. Roll each piece of pastry between sheets of baking paper to make a 5mm (¼-inch) thick, 15cm x 30cm (6-inch x 12-inch) rectangle, trimming edges if necessary. Discard top sheet of baking paper. Transfer pastry and paper attached to base onto each tray. Bake for 12 minutes or until cooked through. Cool.

5 For pumpkin tahini cream, remove skin from roast pumpkin and scoop out 1 cup of pumpkin flesh. Blend or process pumpkin with tahini, garlic and juice. Season.

6 Spread pumpkin tahini cream over pastry leaving a 1cm (½-inch) boarder; top with vegetables. Drizzle with molasses, and sprinkle with sesame seeds and basil. Cut tart in large wedges to serve.

sesame pastry Process flours, sesame seeds and salt until combined. With the motor operating, add oil and the water, 1 tablespoon at a time, until mixture forms a ball and comes away from the side. Divide pastry into two pieces.

TIPS

This tart is delicious served hot or cold. For a short-cut, you can mix the roast pumpkin with store bought hummus.

**NUTRITIONAL
COUNT PER SERVING**
46.1g total fat
6.1g saturated fat
3649kJ (872 cal)
76.2g carbohydrate
27.4g protein
20.8g fibre

NUTRITIONAL
COUNT PER SERVING
10.5g total fat
2.7g saturated fat
671kJ (161 cal)
6.8g carbohydrate
8.3g protein
5.1g fibre

Plus
NUT FREE
YEAST FREE
EGG FREE

Zucchini, pea & PROSCIUTTO SOUP

PREP + COOK TIME 35 MINUTES **SERVES** 6 (MAKES ABOUT 12 CUPS)

- 2 tablespoons olive oil
- 1 large brown onion (200g), chopped
- 2 cloves garlic, sliced
- 4 large zucchini (600g), grated coarsely
- 2 cups (250g) frozen peas
- 100g (3 ounces) kale, shredded
- 1 litre (4 cups) gluten-free chicken or vegetable stock
- 50g (1½ ounces) gluten-free prosciutto
- 50g (1½ ounces) goat's fetta, crumbled

TIPS

Soup is best made on the day of serving. If you want to add more protein to this soup, rinse and drain 400g (12½ ounces) canned cannellini beans; add to soup with peas. Soup can be made to the end of step 3 and frozen for up to 3 months.

1 Heat oil in a large saucepan over medium heat; cook onion, stirring occasionally, for 10 minutes or until soft. Add garlic; cook for 1 minute or until fragrant.

2 Add zucchini and peas; cook, stirring, for 5 minutes or until the zucchini is soft and golden.

3 Stir in kale and stock; bring to the boil, reduce heat to medium-low, simmer, uncovered, for 5 minutes or until kale is wilted. Remove from heat; stand for 10 minutes. Blend or process soup, in batches, until smooth. Season.

4 Preheat grill (broiler). Lightly oil an oven tray. Arrange prosciutto slices on tray. Grill prosciutto for 3 minutes or until crisp and golden on both sides. Drain on paper towel. Break into large pieces.

5 Serve bowls of soup topped with fetta, crisp prosciutto and freshly cracked black pepper, if you like.

Basic gluten-free
4 SEED BREAD

PREP + COOK TIME 1 HOUR 20 MINUTES (+ STANDING) **MAKES** 1 LOAF (12 SLICES)

- 3 cups (405g) gluten-free plain (all-purpose) flour
- ½ cup (75g) potato flour
- ½ cup (80g) brown rice flour
- ½ cup (80g) white rice flour
- 3 teaspoons (10g) dried yeast
- 2 teaspoons salt
- 2 teaspoons xanthan gum
- 1 egg
- 3 egg whites
- ¾ cup (180ml) olive oil
- 1 teaspoon vinegar
- 2 cups (500ml) warm water
- ¼ cup (50g) pepitas (pumpkin seed kernels)
- 2 tablespoons sunflower seeds
- 2 tablespoons linseeds
- 1 tablespoon white chia seeds
- 1 tablespoon olive oil, extra
- 2 teaspoons salt, extra

1 Grease a 11cm x 21.5cm (4½-inch x 8¾-inch) loaf pan; lightly dust with rice flour.

2 Combine sifted flours, yeast, salt and gum in a large bowl.

3 Place egg, egg whites, oil, vinegar and 1½ cups of the warm water in a large bowl of an electric mixer; beat on medium speed for 3½ minutes. Add remaining water and the flour mixture, 1 cup at a time, beating until mixture is combined and smooth. Fold pepitas and seeds through dough.

4 Spoon mixture into loaf pan; smooth the surface. Cover; stand in a warm place for 45 minutes.

5 Preheat oven to 220°C/425°F.

6 Drizzle loaf with extra oil and sprinkle with extra salt. Bake for 1 hour or until crust is firm and golden brown and the loaf sounds hollow when tapped. Stand bread in pan for 5 minutes before turning, top-side up, onto a wire rack to cool. Serve with dairy-free spread, if you like.

TIPS

This bread is best eaten the day it is baked, however, it's great for toast or toasted sandwiches the next day. This mixture will make 6 gluten-free bread rolls – divide dough into six even portions, roll into balls and place on a greased and floured oven tray, then stand 45 minutes. Drizzle rolls with oil and sprinkle with salt; bake for 30 minutes.

Plus
**DAIRY FREE
NUT FREE**

**NUTRITIONAL
COUNT PER SLICE**
20.6g total fat
3g saturated fat
1638kJ (392 cal)
44.4g carbohydrate
5.6g protein
1.6g fibre

4 ways with 4-SEED BREAD

Plus DAIRY FREE NUT FREE

NUTRITIONAL COUNT PER ROLL
32.3g total fat
4.6g saturated fat
2563kJ (613 cal)
68.9g carbohydrate
9g protein
2.4g fibre

Plus DAIRY FREE NUT FREE

NUTRITIONAL COUNT PER WEDGE
15.6g total fat
2.2g saturated fat
1233kJ (295 cal)
33.4g carbohydrate
4.3g protein
1.4g fibre

GARLIC & ROSEMARY COB LOAF

PREP + COOK TIME 1½ HOURS (+ STANDING)

MAKES 1 LOAF (16 WEDGES)

Make basic gluten-free 4-seed bread on page 102 to the end of step 3. Add 4 cloves thinly sliced garlic and ⅓ cup rosemary leaves; fold through dough. Using wet hands shape dough into a 25cm (10-inch) round loaf on an oiled and baking-paper-lined oven tray. Drizzle with 1 tablespoon olive oil and sprinkle with 1 tablespoon rosemary leaves. Cover loaf; stand in a warm place for 45 minutes. Preheat oven to 220°C/425°F. Bake for 50 minutes or until golden in colour and loaf sounds hollow when tapped. Stand loaf on tray for 5 minutes before transferring to a wire rack. Serve warm.

TIPS **If the loaf starts to become too brown, cover with foil. This bread is best eaten on the day it is made. Freeze bread for up to 3 months.**

SEMI-DRIED TOMATO & BASIL ROLLS

PREP + COOK TIME 1½ HOURS (+ STANDING)

MAKES 8 ROLLS

Make basic gluten-free 4-seed bread on page 102 to the end of step 3. Add ⅔ cup thinly sliced drained semi-dried tomatoes and ⅓ cup shredded fresh basil leaves; fold through dough. Divide dough into 8 portions. With wet hands, roll portions into balls. Place on an oiled and baking-paper-lined oven tray. Cover rolls; stand in a warm place for 45 minutes. Preheat oven to 220°C/425°F. Drizzle with 1 tablespoon olive oil. Bake for 40 minutes or until golden in colour and rolls sound hollow when tapped. Stand rolls on tray for 5 minutes before transferring to a wire rack. Serve warm.

TIPS **If the rolls start to become too brown, cover with foil. These rolls are best eaten on the day they are baked. Freeze rolls for up to 3 months.**

NUTRITIONAL COUNT PER ROLL
23.1g total fat
3.4g saturated fat
1745kJ (417 cal)
44.9g carbohydrat
5.8g protein
1.6g fibre

NUTRITIONAL COUNT PER SLICE
12.3g total fat
2.6g saturated fat
909kJ (217 cal)
22.2g carbohydrate
4.3g protein
0.8g fibre

Plus
**DAIRY FREE
NUT FREE**

THREE CHEESE BREAD LOAF

PREP + COOK TIME 1½ HOURS (+ STANDING)

MAKES 2 STICKS (24 SLICES)

Make basic gluten-free 4-seed bread on page 102, to the end of step 3. Add ¼ cup coarsely grated cheddar, ⅓ cup finely grated parmesan and 100g (3 ounces) crumbled fetta; fold through dough. Using damp hands, shape dough into 2 x 35cm (14-inch) long loaves on two oiled and baking-paper-lined trays. Cover loaves; stand in a warm place for 45 minutes. Preheat oven to 220°C/425°F. Drizzle loaves with 1 tablespoon olive oil and sprinkle with 1 teaspoon sea salt flakes. Cut three slits in the top of each loaf. Bake for 55 minutes or until golden in colour and loaf sounds hollow when tapped. Stand loaf on tray for 5 minutes before transferring to a wire rack. Serve warm.

TIPS **This bread is best eaten on the day it is made. Freeze bread for up to 3 months.**

OLIVE & OREGANO PULL-APART ROLLS

PREP + COOK TIME 1½ HOURS (+ STANDING)

MAKES 12 ROLLS

Make basic gluten-free 4-seed bread on page 102 to the end of step 3. Add 1 cup thinly sliced kalamata olives and ⅓ cup chopped oregano leaves; fold through dough. Divide dough into 12 portions. With wet hands, roll portions into balls. Place three rounds, 1cm (½-inch) apart, in centre of an oiled and baking-paper-lined oven tray. Position remaining nine rounds, 1cm (½-inch) apart, in a ring around the edge. Cover rolls, stand in a warm place for 45 minutes. Preheat oven to 220°C/425°F. Drizzle with 1 tablespoon olive oil. Bake for 40 minutes or until golden in colour and rolls sound hollow when tapped. Stand rolls on tray for 5 minutes before transferring to a wire rack. Serve warm.

TIPS **If the rolls start to become too brown, cover with foil. These rolls are best eaten on the day they are baked. Freeze rolls for up to 3 months.**

Pork noodle balls
WITH ASIAN SALAD

PREP + COOK TIME 35 MINUTES (+ STANDING) **SERVES** 4 (MAKES 20 BALLS)

- 50g (1½ ounces) dried mung bean vermicelli
- 500g (1 pound) minced (ground) pork
- 4 green onions (scallions), chopped
- 1 egg white
- 2 tablespoons fish sauce
- 1 teaspoon finely grated lime rind
- 1 tablespoon chopped fresh coriander (cilantro) leaves
- 1 tablespoon coconut oil
- 1 large carrot (180g)
- ¼ medium wombok (napa cabbage) (250g), shredded finely
- 3 kale leaves (100g), stems removed, leaves shredded
- 200g (6½ ounces) cherry tomatoes, halved
- ½ cup loosely packed fresh coriander (cilantro) leaves

DRESSING
- 2 tablespoons rice vinegar
- 2 tablespoons fish sauce
- 2 tablespoons lime juice
- 2 teaspoons coconut sugar
- 2 tablespoons coconut oil, melted
- 2 teaspoons sesame oil

1 Place vermicelli in a small heatproof bowl, cover with boiling water, stand, for 5 minutes or until soft; drain well. Use scissors to cut noodles into shorter lengths.

2 Combine vermicelli, pork, half the green onion, egg white, sauce, rind and chopped coriander in a large bowl. Shape heaped tablespoons of mixture into balls.

3 Heat oil in a large frying pan over a medium heat; cook balls, for 10 minutes, shaking pan occasionally, or until browned all over and cooked through. Transfer to a medium heatproof bowl. Cover to keep warm.

4 Meanwhile, using a vegetable peeler, peel carrot into long thin ribbons. Combine wombok, kale, remaining green onion, carrot, tomato and half the coriander leaves in a large bowl.

5 Make dressing.

6 Pour half the dressing over pork balls; toss to coat. Toss remaining dressing through salad.

7 Serve pork balls on salad topped with remaining coriander leaves.

dressing Whisk ingredients in a small bowl until combined.

TIPS

The pork and noodle balls can be made with chicken or beef, if you prefer. Dressing is best made close to serving, as coconut oil will solidify if made ahead and refrigerated. If it does solidify, stand at room temperature for 30 minutes or warm in 10-second bursts on medium (50%) power in the microwave, stirring, until just melted. Pork balls can be prepared to the end of step 2 a day ahead; keep covered in the fridge.

**NUTRITIONAL
COUNT PER SERVING**
28.3g total fat
17.4g saturated fat
1920kJ (459 cal)
16.9g carbohydrate
31.9g protein
4.9g fibre

Plus

**DAIRY FREE
YEAST FREE**

**NUTRITIONAL
COUNT PER SERVING**
40.3g total fat
11.9g saturated fat
2856kJ (683 cal)
38g carbohydrate
34.5g protein
14.8g fibre

GADO GADO

PREP + COOK TIME 45 MINUTES SERVES 4

- 500g (1 pound) orange sweet potato or white sweet potato, peeled, cut into 3cm (1¼-inch) pieces
- 2 medium carrots (240g), cut into 2cm (¾-inch) thick slices
- 1 small wombok (napa cabbage) (700g), cut lengthways into four wedges
- 200g (6½ ounces) green beans, trimmed
- 200g (6½ ounces) broccolini, cut into long pieces
- 125g (4 ounces) fresh baby corn
- 4 eggs
- 1 tablespoon peanut oil
- 250g (8 ounces) firm tofu or tempeh, cut into 2cm (¾-inch) thick slices, then cut into triangles
- 1¼ cups (100g) bean sprouts, trimmed

PEANUT DRESSING

- ½ cup (140g) smooth natural peanut butter
- 1 tablespoon lime juice
- 1 fresh long red chilli, seeded, chopped finely
- 1 tablespoon tamarind concentrate
- 2 teaspoons coconut sugar
- 400ml can light coconut cream

1 Boil, steam or microwave vegetables, separately, until just tender.

2 Meanwhile, bring a small saucepan of water to the boil. Add eggs; boil for 9 minutes. Drain; rinse under cold water until cool enough to handle. Peel eggs, halve.

3 Make peanut dressing.

4 Heat oil in a large frying pan; cook tofu for 3 minutes on each side or until golden.

5 Arrange vegetables, sprouts, eggs and tofu on a platter or plates. Drizzle with peanut dressing. Serve topped with fried shallots or roasted salted peanuts, if you like.

peanut dressing Combine peanut butter, juice, chilli, tamarind, sugar and coconut cream in a small saucepan; cook, stirring, over low heat until sugar dissolves. Bring to the boil; cook, stirring, for 5 minutes or until thickened. (If you like a thinner peanut sauce, stir in ½ cup water while heating). Cover to keep warm.

TIPS

You can substitute your favourite vegetables in this recipe. Peanut dressing can be made a day ahead; keep covered in the fridge. Reheat before serving and add a little water if the consistancy is too thick.

Niçoise salad with
TUNA DILL PATTIES

PREP + COOK TIME 1 HOUR **SERVES** 4

- 1 large (300g) potato, quartered
- 300g (10 ounces) green beans, trimmed
- 425g (13½ ounces) canned tuna in olive oil, drained
- 2 green onions (scallions), chopped
- 2 tablespoons chopped fresh dill
- 1 teaspoon finely grated lemon rind
- 2 tablespoons lemon juice
- 1 tablespoon dijon mustard
- 1 egg, beaten lightly
- ¼ cup (35g) buckwheat flour
- 2 tablespoons olive oil
- 4 eggs
- 200g (6½ ounces) small cherry tomatoes, halved
- 4 medium red radish (80g), sliced
- 1 cup (120g) sicilian green olives
- 1 medium lemon (140g), cut into wedges
- dill sprigs, to serve

DILL DRESSING

- 2 tablespoons verjuice
- 1 tablespoon dijon mustard
- 1 teaspoon honey
- 1 tablespoon chopped fresh dill
- ¼ cup (60ml) olive oil

1 Boil, steam or microwave potato until soft. Transfer to a large heatproof bowl; mash until smooth.

2 Boil, steam or microwave beans until just tender. Refresh under cold water; drain.

3 Add tuna, green onions, dill, rind, juice, mustard, beaten egg and flour to potato; mix well to combine. Season. Divide mixture into eight patties.

4 Heat oil in a large frying pan over a medium heat; cook patties, for 3 minutes each side or until browned. Drain on paper towel.

5 Meanwhile, bring a small saucepan of water to the boil. Add eggs; boil for 5 minutes. Drain; rinse under cold water until cool enough to handle. Peel eggs; halve.

6 Make dill dressing.

7 Place beans, tomato, radish and olives in a bowl with half the dressing; toss gently to combine.

8 Serve patties with salad, egg and lemon; drizzle with remaining dressing, top with dill sprigs.

dill dressing Whisk ingredients in a small bowl until combined. Season.

These patties are delicious used as fillings for burgers or in gluten-free wraps.

Plus
**NUT FREE
YEAST FREE
EGG FREE**

NUTRITIONAL
COUNT PER SERVING
31g total fat
11g saturated fat
3367kJ (805 cal)
79g carbohydrate
32g protein
17g fibre

Buckwheat risotto with
TOMATO, FENNEL & HALOUMI

PREP + COOK TIME 40 MINUTES (+ STANDING) **SERVES** 4

You will need to start this recipe a day ahead.

- 2 cups (400g) buckwheat
- 2 tablespoons olive oil
- 1 large red onion (300g), chopped
- 1 small fennel bulb (200g), sliced thinly
- 2 cloves garlic, chopped
- 1 cup (250ml) white wine
- ½ cup (125ml) gluten-free vegetable stock
- 800g (1½ pounds) canned diced tomatoes
- 2 tablespoons drained capers
- 300g (9½ ounces) haloumi, torn
- ⅔ cup (110g) kalamata olives
- 2 cups (90g) shredded kale
- 2 tablespoons fresh baby basil leaves

1 Place buckwheat in a medium bowl; cover with cold water. Stand overnight. Rinse buckwheat under cold running water until the water runs clear. Drain.

2 Heat oil in a large frying pan over medium heat. Add onion and fennel; cook, stirring occasionally, for 10 minutes or until soft and golden.

3 Add garlic; cook, stirring, for 1 minute or until fragrant. Add buckwheat; cook, stirring, for 5 minutes.

4 Add wine to pan; bring to the boil; cook, stirring, over high heat for 5 minutes or until wine has evaporated. Stir in combined stock and tomatoes; cook, covered, over low heat 10 minutes or until buckwheat is just tender and liquid has been absorbed.

5 Stir in capers, haloumi and olives; cook, covered, for 5 minutes or until haloumi is soft. Add kale; cook, stirring, for 3 minutes or until bright green.

6 Serve risotto topped with basil leaves.

TIPS

This recipe can be made with arborio rice if you do not have buckwheat; you will need to gradually add about 2 cups gluten-free stock in step 4, or until rice is tender.

Nourishing vegetable bowl
WITH GINGER BROWN RICE

PREP + COOK TIME 1 HOUR **SERVES** 4

- 400g (12½ ounces) jap pumpkin, skin on
- 1½ cups (300g) medium-grain brown rice
- 1 tablespoon grated fresh ginger
- 1 teaspoon sesame oil
- 1 tablespoon tamari
- 3 cups (750ml) water
- 200g (6½ ounces) broccoli, cut into large florets
- ⅔ cup (120g) shelled edamame
- 200g (6½ ounces) kale, trimmed, chopped coarsely
- 1 cup (200g) red superkraut (see tips), drained
- 1 medium avocado (250g), sliced
- ½ cup (75g) mixed seeds (see tips)

TAMARI DRESSING

- ½ cup (140g) hulled tahini, at room temperature
- 2 tablespoons apple cider vinegar
- 1 tablespoon tamari
- 1 tablespoon gluten-free white (shiro) miso
- ⅓ cup (80ml) water, approximately

1 Preheat oven to 200°C/400°F. Line an oven tray with baking paper.

2 Place pumpkin on tray; bake for 45 minutes or until tender. Cool slightly; cut into thick wedges.

3 Meanwhile, place rice, ginger, oil, tamari and the water in a medium saucepan; bring to the boil. Reduce heat to low; cook, covered, for 30 minutes or until rice is tender and liquid is absorbed.

4 Meanwhile, make tamari dressing.

5 Boil, steam or microwave broccoli, edamame and kale, separately, until just tender. Refresh under cold water; drain.

6 Divide rice between four bowls. Arrange pumpkin, kraut, avocado, broccoli, kale and edamame over rice. Drizzle tamari dressing over each bowl; sprinkle with mixed seeds. Serve with remaining dressing.

tamari dressing Whisk tahini, vinegar, tamari and miso in a small bowl until combined. Whisk in enough of the water to form a pouring consistency.

TIPS

We used red "superkraut", a variation on sauerkraut, that contains cabbage, beetroot and bush tomato. It's available in the refrigerator section of some health food stores. Store in the refrigerator and take care when opening; it can sometimes fizz or bubble. If unavailable, use regular sauerkraut, kimchi or pickled beetroot if you prefer. We used a mixture of pepitas (pumpkin seed kernels), sunflower seeds and sesame seeds.

Plus
NUT FREE
DAIRY FREE
YEAST FREE
EGG FREE

NUTRITIONAL
COUNT PER SERVING
46.6g total fat
6.8g saturated fat
3536kJ (846 cal)
72.3g carbohydrate
26.7g protein
11.4g fibre

**NUTRITIONAL
COUNT PER CRACKER**
21.5g total fat
6.3g saturated fat
1099kJ (263 cal)
8.3g carbohydrate
9.5g protein
0.8g fibre

Plus
**YEAST FREE
NUT FREE**

Sesame tahini CRACKERS

PREP + COOK TIME 35 MINUTES MAKES 8

- ½ cup (140g) hulled tahini, at room temperature
- 40g (1½ ounces) butter or coconut oil, melted
- 2 eggs, beaten lightly
- 1 tablespoon gluten-free miso or wholegrain mustard
- ⅓ cup (50g) sesame seeds
- ½ cup (80g) coconut flour

TIPS

Crackers can be kept in an airtight container in a cool dry place for up to 1 week.

1 Preheat oven to 180°C/350°F. Grease and line a baking tray with baking paper.

2 Place tahini in a medium bowl. Add butter, egg, miso, seeds, pinch sea salt and flour; stir until well combined. Gather mixture together with hands.

3 Roll mixture between sheets of baking paper until a 33cm x 23cm (13¼-inch x 9-inch) rectangle. Remove top sheet of paper; trim edges to neaten to 32cm x 22cm (12¾-inch x 8¾-inch). Cut dough into eight 11cm x 8cm (4½-inch x 3¼-inch) rectangular crackers. Place on tray 2cm (¾-inch) apart.

4 Bake for 13 minutes or until crisp and golden; the edges will brown faster than the middle. Cool on trays.

4 ways with CRACKERS

NUTRITIONAL COUNT PER CRACKER WITH TOPPING
23g total fat
7.1g saturated fat
1250kJ (299 cal)
8.7g carbohydrate
14.4g protein
0.9g fibre

Plus
YEAST FREE NUT FREE

Plus
YEAST FREE NUT FREE

NUTRITIONAL COUNT PER CRACKER WITH TOPPING
25.4g total fat
8.5g saturated fat
1314kJ (314 cal)
8.7g carbohydrate
13.3g protein
0.8g fibre

CREAM CHEESE, SMOKED SALMON & DILL PICKLES

PREP + COOK TIME 40 MINUTES MAKES 8

Make 1 quantity of sesame tahini crackers on page 117. Top the crackers with 80g (2½oz) softened cream cheese, 100g (3oz) smoked salmon, 50g (1½oz) sliced dill pickles and 1 tablespoon chopped fresh chives.

LEMON RICOTTA, TUNA & ROCKET

PREP + COOK TIME 40 MINUTES MAKES 8

Make 1 quantity of sesame tahini crackers on page 117. Top the crackers with 80g (2½oz) fresh ricotta combined with 1 teaspoon finely grated lemon rind, 185g (6oz) canned drained tuna in springwater, 30g (1oz) baby rocket (arugula). Season; serve with lemon wedges.

NUTRITIONAL COUNT PER CRACKER WITH TOPPING
25.4g total fat
8.6g saturated fat
1363kJ (326 cal)
8.8g carbohydrate
15.6g protein
1.1g fibre

Plus
YEAST FREE NUT FREE

NUTRITIONAL COUNT PER CRACKER WITH TOPPING
29.6g total fat
8.2g saturated fat
1464kJ (350 cal)
8.9g carbohydrate
12g protein
1.5g fibre

Plus
YEAST FREE NUT FREE

JARLSBERG, HAM & QUICK VINEGAR TOMATOES

PREP + COOK TIME 45 MINUTES   MAKES 8

Make 1 quantity of sesame tahini crackers on page 117. Slice 2 medium ripe roma tomatoes; place in a shallow bowl, drizzle with 1 tablespoon sherry vinegar; stand 5 minutes. Top the crackers with 100g (3oz) sliced jarlsberg cheese, 100g (3oz) shaved leg ham and drained tomato slices. Season.

AVOCADO, TURKEY, ALFALFA & POMEGRANATE

PREP + COOK TIME 40 MINUTES   MAKES 8

Make 1 quantity of sesame tahini crackers on page 117. Top the crackers with 1 halved, sliced large avocado, 100g (3oz) thinly sliced turkey, 20g (¾oz) alfalfa sprouts and 1 tablespoon pomegranate seeds.

MAIN MEALS

Peanut-free satay
CHICKEN SKEWERS

PREP + COOK TIME 30 MINUTES SERVES 4

You need to cook ⅔ cup jasmine rice for the amount of cooked rice in this recipe.

- ⅓ cup (95g) nut-free butter (see tips)
- 270ml canned coconut milk
- 2 tablespoons tamari
- 2 tablespoons sweet chilli sauce
- 2 tablespoons lime juice
- 2 tablespoons tamari, extra
- 1 teaspoon sweet chilli sauce, extra
- 12 chicken tenderloins (640g)
- 200g (6½ ounces) snow peas, trimmed
- 170g (5½ ounces) broccolini
- 2 cups (300g) cooked jasmine rice
- 2 tablespoons fresh coriander (cilantro) leaves
- 1 teaspoon toasted sesame seeds

1 Heat a small heavy-based saucepan over medium heat; cook nut-free butter and coconut milk, without boiling, stirring until smooth. Stir in tamari, sweet chilli sauce and juice; cook, stirring for 1 minute or until hot.

2 Combine extra tamari and extra sweet chilli sauce in a small bowl. Thread chicken onto 12 skewers; season. Cook chicken on a heated oiled grill pan (or barbecue or grill) for about 2 minutes each side or until cooked through; brush with half the tamari mixture in the final minute of cooking.

3 Meanwhile, boil, steam or microwave snow peas and broccolini, separately, until just tender.

4 Arrange snow peas and broccolini on a serving platter; drizzle with remaining tamari mixture. Top with chicken, serve with rice and satay sauce. Sprinkle with coriander and sesame seeds.

TIPS

We used a peanut-butter-style, nut-free butter made from roasted sunflower seeds; available smooth and crunchy, from health food stores, some larger supermarkets and online.

Plus
**NUT FREE
DAIRY FREE
EGG FREE**

**NUTRITIONAL
COUNT PER SERVING**
35g total fat
16.5g saturated fat
2737kJ (654 cal)
36.8g carbohydrate
46.1g protein
2.9g fibre

Plus
**YEAST FREE
NUT FREE**

**NUTRITIONAL
COUNT PER BURGER**
21g total fat
3.4g saturated fat
1605kJ (383 cal)
23.6g carbohydrate
22g protein
6.3g fibre

Sweet potato TURKEY BURGERS

PREP + COOK TIME 1 HOUR (+ REFRIGERATION) **MAKES** 6

The sweet potato needs to be about 12cm (4¾ inches) in diameter, as it will serve as the 'bun' for the burgers.

- 1 large orange sweet potato (500g), unpeeled
- cooking-oil spray
- ⅓ cup (25g) quinoa flakes
- ¼ cup (60ml) milk
- 1 small zucchini (90g), grated coarsely
- 1 small purple carrot (70g), grated coarsely
- 1 small red onion (100g), grated coarsely
- 400g (12½ ounces) minced (ground) free-range turkey or chicken
- 1 tablespoon finely chopped fresh flat-leaf parsley
- 2 tablespoons olive oil
- 1 large tomato (220g), sliced thinly
- 1 small red onion (100g), extra, sliced thinly
- 60g (2 ounces) trimmed watercress
- 1 tablespoon sesame seeds, toasted

GREEN TAHINI

- ¼ cup (70g) tahini
- 2 tablespoons fresh flat-leaf parsley leaves
- 2 tablespoons lemon juice
- 1 tablespoon olive oil
- 1 small clove garlic, crushed

1 Preheat oven to 200°C/400°F. Oil and line two large oven trays with baking paper.

2 Cut sweet potato into 12 x 1.5cm (¾-inch) thick rounds; discard tapered ends. Place sweet potato slices, in a single layer, on oven trays; spray with cooking oil. Roast for 20 minutes or until tender. Cover to keep warm.

3 Meanwhile, make green tahini.

4 Combine quinoa flakes and milk in a small bowl; stand for 10 minutes.

5 Combine zucchini, carrot, onion, turkey, parsley and quinoa mixture in a medium bowl; season to taste. Using damp hands, shape turkey mixture into six 8cm (3¼-inch) patties. Cover, refrigerate for 30 minutes.

6 Heat oil in a large non-stick frying pan over medium heat; cook patties for 4 minutes on each side or until golden and cooked through.

7 Place patties on six sweet potato rounds; top with tomato, extra onion, watercress, green tahini and remaining sweet potato rounds. Sprinkle with sesame seeds.

green tahini Process ingredients until smooth; season.

Salt & pepper SQUID

PREP + COOK TIME 35 MINUTES SERVES 4

- 2 tablespoons sea salt
- 2 tablespoons black peppercorns
- 1½ teaspoons dried chilli flakes
- ¼ cup (35g) 100% corn (maize) cornflour (cornstarch)
- vegetable oil, for deep frying
- 750g (1½ pounds) cleaned squid hoods, sliced thinly
- 125g (4 ounces) mixed baby salad leaves
- 1 lebanese cucumber (130g), halved, sliced thinly
- ½ small red onion (50g), sliced thinly
- 1 small carrot (70g), cut into matchsticks
- 1 tablespoon rice wine vinegar
- 2 teaspoons light olive oil

1 Crush salt, peppercorns and chilli with a mortar and pestle; combine with cornflour in a medium bowl.

2 Heat vegetable oil in a large heavy-based saucepan over medium-high heat until oil reaches 190°C/375°F on a sugar (candy) thermometer (or when a cube of bread turns golden in about 10 seconds).

3 Coat squid in cornflour mixture; shake off excess. Deep-fry squid, in batches, for 3 minutes or until lightly browned and cooked through. Drain on paper towel; cover to keep warm.

4 Place salad leaves and remaining ingredients in a large bowl; toss gently to combine. Transfer salad to a large serving platter; top with squid. Serve with lemon wedges, if you like.

TIPS

To save you time, ask the fishmonger to clean the squid hoods for you. This recipe is best made just before serving.

**NUTRITIONAL
COUNT PER SERVING**
26.7g total fat
9.3g saturated fat
2157kJ (516 cal)
38.6g carbohydrate
27.7g protein
6.3g fibre

Mushroom, cavolo nero & QUINOA RISOTTO

PREP + COOK TIME 45 MINUTES **SERVES** 4

- 10g (½ ounce) dried porcini mushrooms
- ½ cup (125ml) boiling water
- 200g (6 ounces) button mushrooms
- 2 tablespoons olive oil
- 1 medium brown onion (150g), chopped finely
- 1 flat mushroom (80g), chopped coarsely
- 2 cloves garlic, crushed
- 1 cup quinoa (200g), rinsed, drained
- 1.25 litres (5 cups) gluten-free vegetable stock
- 1 sprig fresh thyme
- 100g (3 ounces) cavolo nero (tuscan cabbage), sliced thinly
- 120g (4 ounces) goat's cheese, crumbled
- ⅓ cup (25g) finely grated parmesan

1 Place porcini mushrooms in a heatproof bowl with the boiling water. Stand for 5 minutes.

2 Meanwhile, cut half of the button mushrooms in half; leave remaining whole. Heat oil in a medium frying pan over medium heat; cook onion, stirring, for 3 minutes or until soft. Add flat and button mushrooms; cook, stirring, for 3 minutes or until browned and tender. Add garlic; cook, stirring, for 1 minute or until fragrant.

3 Stir in quinoa, stock and thyme. Remove porcini mushrooms from water (reserve the soaking liquid); chop coarsely. Add porcini and soaking liquid to pan; bring to the boil. Simmer, uncovered, for 20 minutes until liquid is absorbed and quinoa is tender. Discard thyme. Add cavolo nero; stir until wilted. Remove pan from heat; stir in goat's cheese and half the parmesan.

4 Serve risotto topped with remaining parmesan. Season with pepper.

serving suggestion Serve topped with a poached egg.

Pancetta & mushroom
CRÊPES WITH TOMATO SAUCE

PREP + COOK TIME 1½ HOURS **SERVES** 4

- 1 tablespoon olive oil
- 1 large brown onion (200g), chopped finely
- 2 cloves garlic, crushed
- 400g (12½ ounces) canned diced tomatoes
- 2 tablespoons finely shredded fresh basil
- 200g (6½ ounces) button mushrooms, sliced thinly
- 50g (1½ ounces) mild pancetta, chopped coarsely
- 500g (1 pound) fresh ricotta
- 250g (8 ounces) frozen spinach, thawed, drained
- 1 cup (100g) coarsely grated mozzarella
- micro basil, optional

GLUTEN-FREE CRÊPES
- 2 eggs
- ½ cup (65g) gluten-free plain (all-purpose) flour
- ¼ cup (45g) rice flour
- ¾ cup (180ml) milk
- 40g (1½ ounces) butter, melted

1 Make gluten-free crêpes.

2 Heat half the oil in a large frying pan over medium heat; cook onion and garlic, stirring, for 5 minutes or until onion softens. Add tomatoes; cook, uncovered, over low heat, stirring occasionally, for 5 minutes or until sauce thickens slightly. Remove from heat. Cool slightly. Stir in basil; season to taste.

3 Heat remaining oil in a medium frying pan over high heat; cook mushrooms and pancetta, stirring, for 5 minutes or until softened. Transfer to a medium bowl; stir in ricotta and spinach. Season to taste.

4 Preheat oven to 180°C/350°F.

5 Spoon half the tomato sauce over the base of a 2 litre (8-cup) ovenproof dish. Divide ricotta mixture evenly between crêpes; roll to enclose. Arrange crêpes, side-by-side, in dish. Spoon over remaining tomato sauce; sprinkle with mozzarella.

6 Bake, uncovered, for 20 minutes or until mixture is heated through and mozzarella is golden. Serve topped with micro basil, if you like.

gluten-free crêpes Whisk eggs in a medium bowl; add flours, whisk to combine. Gradually add milk, whisking between additions until batter is smooth; season. Heat a 20cm (8-inch) (base measurement) frying pan over medium heat; brush with melted butter. Pour 2 tablespoonfuls of batter into pan; swirl to coat base. Cook for 1 minute or until golden; turn, cook for a further 30 seconds. Repeat to make a total of eight crêpes.

TIPS

Crêpes can be made a day ahead; store in an airtight container. Swap pancetta for gluten-free bacon or ham, if you like. Fresh ricotta is available from the deli section of supermarkets.

Plus
**YEAST FREE
NUT FREE**

**NUTRITIONAL
COUNT PER SERVING**
46.7g total fat
15.8g saturated fat
3693kJ (883 cal)
48.9g carbohydrate
55.6g protein
10.3g fibre

Prosciutto & rosemary
ROAST CHICKEN

PREP + COOK TIME 2 HOURS (+ REFRIGERATION) **SERVES** 4

- 1.6kg (3¼-pound) free-range chicken
- 2 trimmed celery sticks (200g),
  cut into 2cm (¾-inch) pieces
- 2 medium carrots (240g), cut into 2cm (¾-inch) pieces
- 2 small leeks (400g), cut into 2cm (¾-inch) pieces
- 2 medium brown onions (300g), cut into wedges
- 1 bulb garlic (70g), halved
- 2 tablespoons olive oil
- 1 cup (250ml) white wine
- 2 tablespoons 100% corn (maize) cornflour (cornstarch)
- 2 tablespoons water
- 2 cups (500ml) gluten-free chicken stock

PROSCIUTTO & ROSEMARY STUFFING
- 40g (1½ ounces) butter
- 1 small leek (200g) sliced thinly
- 2 cloves garlic, crushed
- 8 slices gluten-free prosciutto (120g), chopped finely
- 2 cups (140g) stale gluten-free breadcrumbs (see tips)
- 1 tablespoon finely chopped fresh rosemary

TIPS

Place gluten-free bread in a single layer in a wire rack to dry out and go stale, otherwise lightly toast to make dry before processing. You can always blend the gravy and leave the vegetables in for a thicker, richer gravy.

1 Preheat oven to 200°C/400°F.

2 Make prosciutto and rosemary stuffing.

3 Rinse chicken under cold water; pat dry inside and out with paper towel. Fill chicken cavity with stuffing. Tie legs with kitchen string, place chicken in a large metal baking dish with celery, carrots, leek, onion and garlic. Drizzle oil over chicken and vegetables, season.

4 Bake for 15 minutes. Reduce oven to 180°C/350°F; bake for a further 1¼ hours or until the juices run clear when the thickest part of the chicken thigh is pierced with a skewer. Transfer chicken to a large plate or serving platter. Cover with foil; rest for 15 minutes.

5 Squeeze garlic from skin over vegetables. Mash vegetables and garlic until smooth in the baking dish. Place dish over medium heat, add wine; cook, stirring, until combined. Increase heat to high; cook until the wine is evaporated.

6 Stir in blended cornflour and the water, gradually stir in stock; cook, stirring until the gravy boils and thickens. Strain the vegetable mixture over a large jug. Discard vegetable mixture. Reserve the gravy.

7 Serve chicken with gravy and roasted vegetables, if you like.

prosciutto & rosemary stuffing Heat butter in a medium frying pan over high heat; cook leek, garlic and prosciutto, stirring for 5 minutes or until leek is tender. Stir in breadcrumbs; cook for 2 minutes or until toasted lightly. Remove from heat; stir in rosemary. Season, cool.

Haloumi & vegetable
KEBABS ON SPECKLED QUINOA

PREP + COOK TIME 20 MINUTES (+ REFRIGERATION) SERVES 4

- 4 medium lemons (560g)
- 450g (14½ ounces) haloumi, cut into 3cm (1¼-inch) pieces
- 200g (6½ ounces) cherry tomatoes
- 3 medium zucchini (360g), cut into thick slices
- 2 green onions (scallions), cut into 3cm (1¼-inch) pieces
- 2 cloves garlic, crushed
- ¼ cup fresh thyme leaves, chopped
- ⅓ cup (80ml) verjuice
- ¼ cup (60ml) extra virgin olive oil
- 3 cups (750ml) water
- 1 cup (200g) tricolour quinoa
- 20g (¾ ounce) butter
- 2 tablespoons finely chopped preserved lemon rind
- 2 tablespoons chopped fresh flat-leaf parsley

TIPS

If using bamboo skewers, first soak overnight in cold water. Vegetable mixture can be marinated up to 8 hours ahead. Speckled quinoa can be cooked up to 8 hours ahead; reheat just before serving.

1 Cut two lemons into 16 wedges. Finely grate rind and squeeze juice from remaining two lemons; you will need 2 teaspoons rind and ⅓ cup (80ml) juice.

2 Place haloumi, tomatoes, zucchini, green onions and lemon wedges in a glass bowl.

3 Whisk rind, juice, garlic, thyme, verjuice and oil in a small bowl; pour half over vegetables; toss to combine. Cover; refrigerate for 2 hours. Reserve remaining marinade.

4 Bring the water to the boil in a medium saucepan. Rinse quinoa under cold running water until liquid runs clear; drain well. Add quinoa to pan; simmer, uncovered, for 15 minutes or until tender, drain well. Return quinoa to same pan; stir in butter, preserved lemon and parsley. Season. Cover to keep warm.

5 Meanwhile, thread haloumi, vegetables and lemon wedges onto 8 oiled skewers. Cook skewers on a baking-paper-lined grill plate (or grill or barbecue), for 2 minutes each side or until haloumi is golden and vegetables are tender. Brush with marinade during cooking.

6 Serve skewers with speckled quinoa. Drizzle with reserved marinade.

**NUTRITIONAL
COUNT PER SERVING**
40.5g total fat
17.7g saturated fat
2865kJ (986 cal)
41.2g carbohydrate
32.8g protein
7.7g fibre

**NUTRITIONAL
COUNT PER SERVING**
23.7g total fat
6.8g saturated fat
1565kJ (374 cal)
19.4g carbohydrate
18.9g protein
6.2g fibre

Smoky bean & beef burgers
WITH AVOCADO SMASH

PREP + COOK TIME 40 MINUTES (+ REFRIGERATION) **SERVES** 6

- 300g (9½ ounces) minced (ground) beef
- 400g (12½ ounces) canned red kidney beans, drained, rinsed, mashed coarsely
- 1 teaspoon smoked paprika
- 1 teaspoon ground cumin
- ¼ cup (30g) coarsely grated cheddar
- 1 medium red onion (170g), grated coarsely
- 1 clove garlic, crushed
- 1 egg
- 1 cup (70g) crushed gluten-free plain rice crackers
- 2 tablespoons olive oil
- 4 small ripe tomatoes (360g), chopped
- 2 tablespoons chopped fresh coriander (cilantro) leaves
- 2 small avocados (400g)
- 1 tablespoon lime juice
- 1 iceberg lettuce leaves
- ½ teaspoon smoked paprika, extra

1 Combine beef, beans, paprika, cumin, cheddar, onion, garlic, egg and crackers in a large bowl; season. Shape mixture into six flat patties. Refrigerate for 30 minutes or until firm.

2 Heat oil in a large frying pan over a medium heat; cook patties, for 5 minutes each side or until browned and cooked through. Remove from heat; cover to keep warm.

3 Meanwhile, combine tomato and coriander in a small bowl; season to taste.

4 Mash avocado and juice together in a medium bowl until smooth and creamy; season.

5 Remove outer leaves from lettuce, cut lettuce in half then separate leaves to give six rounds.

6 Serve patties on lettuce leaves topped with avocado and tomato mixture, sprinkled with a little extra smoked paprika.

TIPS

The patties can be made to the end of step 2 a day ahead, or frozen for up to 2 months.

Polenta gnocchi with
GARLIC MUSHROOMS

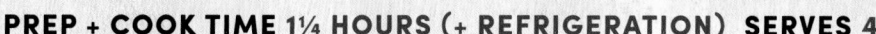

PREP + COOK TIME 1¼ HOURS (+ REFRIGERATION) **SERVES 4**

- 10g (½ ounce) dried sliced porcini mushrooms
- ½ cup (125ml) boiling water
- 1 tablespoon olive oil
- 30g (1 ounce) butter
- 1 medium leek (350g), sliced thinly
- 2 cloves garlic, sliced
- 200g (6½ ounces) flat mushrooms, sliced thinly
- 100g (3 ounces) swiss brown mushrooms, sliced thinly
- 150g (4½ ounces) mixed mushrooms (see tips)
- 1 cup (250ml) white wine
- 1 tablespoon torn fresh sage leaves
- 300ml light thickened (heavy) cream
- 1 cup (250ml) gluten-free vegetable stock
- 60g (2 ounces) baby spinach leaves
- 2 tablespoons grated parmesan

POLENTA GNOCCHI

- 2 cups (500ml) milk
- 2 cups (500ml) gluten-free chicken stock
- 1 cups (170g) instant polenta (cornmeal)
- 25g (¾ ounces) butter, chopped
- ½ cup (40g) finely grated parmesan

1 Make polenta gnocchi.

2 Combine porcini mushrooms and the water in a small heatproof bowl; stand for 10 minutes.

3 Meanwhile, heat oil and butter in a large frying pan over medium heat; cook leek, stirring occasionally, for 5 minutes or until soft and golden. Add garlic and mushrooms; cook, stirring occasionally, for 5 minutes or until mushrooms soften.

4 Add wine; bring to the boil. Boil, uncovered, until wine is evaporated. Stir in sage, cream, stock and porcini mushrooms with liquid. Bring to the boil; reduce heat, simmer, uncovered, for 10 minutes or until sauce thickens slightly. Remove from heat, stir in half the spinach; season.

5 Serve gnocchi topped with mushroom sauce, remaining spinach leaves and parmesan.

polenta gnocchi Grease and line a deep 20cm (8-inch) square cake pan with baking paper. Combine milk and stock in a medium saucepan; bring to the boil. Gradually add polenta, stirring constantly. Reduce heat; cook, stirring, for 5 minutes or until polenta is soft and creamy. Stir in butter and half the parmesan until combined. Pour mixture into pan. Refrigerate for 30 minutes or until set. Preheat grill (broiler) to high. Cut polenta into 9cm (3¾-inch) rounds. Place on an oiled oven tray, sprinkle with remaining cheese; place under grill for 5 minutes or until golden and crisp.

TIPS

We used a combination of oyster, enoki and shimeji mushrooms in this recipe. Dried porcini are available in delis. They can be omitted, but do give an intense mushroom flavour. Polenta gnocchi can be made a day ahead; reheat in oven.

Plus
**NUT FREE
YEAST FREE
EGG FREE**

**NUTRITIONAL
COUNT PER SERVING**
39.4g total fat
22.2g saturated fat
2773kJ (663 cal)
46.5g carbohydrate
22g protein
6.9g fibre

Plus

**NUT FREE
YEAST FREE
EGG FREE**

**NUTRITIONAL
COUNT PER SERVING**
27.6g total fat
11.4g saturated fat
2344kJ (561 cal)
44.7g carbohydrate
29.6g protein
7.1g fibre

Quinoa & buckwheat
MARGHERITA PIZZA

PREP + COOK TIME 45 MINUTES (+ STANDING) **SERVES** 2

- 1 teaspoon olive oil
- 2 tablespoons white chia seeds
- ⅓ cup (80ml) water
- ⅔ cup (110g) white quinoa, rinsed
- 1½ tablespoons buckwheat flour
- 1 teaspoon gluten-free baking powder
- 1½ tablespoons finely grated parmesan
- a pinch of salt
- ⅓ cup (80ml) water, extra
- ½ cup (125ml) passata
- 2 tablespoons finely shredded fresh basil leaves
- ¼ cup (20g) finely grated parmesan, extra
- 100g (3 ounces) bocconcini, torn
- ¼ cup loosely packed fresh basil leaves, extra

1 Preheat oven to 220°C/425°F. Line a 30cm (12-inch) round pizza tray with baking paper; brush paper with oil.

2 Combine chia seeds and the water in a small bowl. Stand for 10 minutes or until thick.

3 Place quinoa, flour, baking powder, parmesan, salt, extra water and chia mixture in a high-powered blender. Blend until almost smooth, stopping the blender and scraping down the sides several times during blending. Spread mixture evenly over tray.

4 Bake pizza base for 15 minutes or until firm, crisp and golden brown.

5 Spread combined passata and shredded basil on pizza base leaving a 1cm (½-inch) border. Top with extra parmesan and the bocconcini.

6 Bake pizza for 10 minutes or until cheeses are golden and bubbling. Sprinkle with extra basil leaves and cracked pepper, if you like.

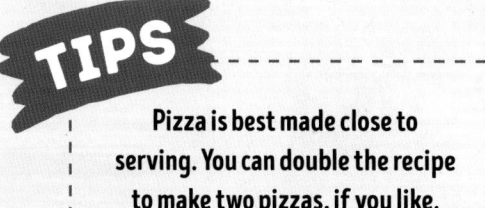

TIPS

Pizza is best made close to serving. You can double the recipe to make two pizzas, if you like.

4 ways with PIZZA BASE

NUTRITIONAL COUNT PER SERVING
39.5g total fat
17g saturated fat
3115kJ (745 cal)
45.3g carbohydrate
48.6g protein
7.4g fibre

Plus
**NUT FREE
YEAST FREE
EGG FREE**

Plus
**YEAST FREE
EGG FREE**

NUTRITIONAL COUNT PER SERVING
39.9g total fat
15.7g saturated fat
3096kJ (741 cal)
55.8g carbohydrate
36.9g protein
8.5g fibre

ROCKET, PROSCIUTTO & PARMESAN PIZZA

PREP + COOK TIME 45 MINUTES
(+ STANDING) **SERVES** 2

Make pizza base using recipe on page 141 to the end of step 5. Bake for 10 minutes or until cheese is golden and bubbling. Top with 100g (3oz) thinly sliced gluten-free prosciutto, 30g (1oz) baby rocket (arugula) and 2 tablespoons shaved parmesan.

CHAR-GRILLED VEG, PESTO & GOAT'S CHEESE PIZZA

PREP + COOK TIME 1 HOUR
(+ STANDING) **SERVES** 2

Make pizza base using recipe on page 141 to the end of step 5. Cook lightly oiled 100g (3oz) sliced orange sweet potato and 50g (1½oz) sliced zucchini on a heated oiled grill plate (or grill or barbecue) for 3 minutes each side or until vegetables are tender. Top pizza with 100g (3oz) thinly sliced drained chargrilled red capsicum (bell pepper) (see tip), chargrilled vegetables and 50g (1½oz) crumbled marinated goat's cheese. Bake for 10 minutes or until cheese is golden and bubbling. Serve topped with 1 tablespoon basil pesto.

TIP Pat capsicum dry with paper towel.

**NUTRITIONAL
COUNT PER SERVING**
29.6g total fat
12.1g saturated fat
2674kJ (616 cal)
49g carbohydrate
39.7g protein
8.5g fibre

Plus
**NUT FREE
YEAST FREE
EGG FREE**

Plus
**NUT FREE
YEAST FREE
EGG FREE**

**NUTRITIONAL
COUNT PER SERVING**
53.3g total fat
21g saturated fat
3620kJ (866 cal)
50.8g carbohydrate
41.1g protein
8.3g fibre

HAM, PINEAPPLE & CHILLI PIZZA

PREP + COOK TIME 45 MINUTES
(+ STANDING) SERVES 2

Make pizza base using recipe on page 141 to the end of step 5. Top pizza with 100g (3oz) thinly sliced gluten-free leg ham, 100g (3oz) thinly sliced pineapple and ½ teaspoon chilli flakes. Bake for 10 minutes or until the cheese is golden and bubbling.

TIP **Omit chilli flakes, if you like.**

SALAMI, BLUE CHEESE & ONION PIZZA

PREP + COOK TIME 1 HOUR
(+ STANDING) SERVES 2

Heat 2 teaspoons olive oil in a large frying pan over low heat; cook 1 thinly sliced red onion, stirring occasionally, for 10 minutes or until golden brown. Add 1 teaspoon brown sugar; stir until dissolved. Make pizza base using recipe on page 141 to the end of step 5. Top pizza with 50g (1½oz) crumbled creamy blue cheese, 50g (1½oz) thinly sliced spicy gluten-free salami, 50g (1½oz) pitted kalamata olives and the caramelised onion. Bake for 10 minutes or until the cheese is golden and bubbling.

Spiced lamb & sweet potato
WITH TURMERIC QUINOA

PREP + COOK TIME 1 HOUR **SERVES** 4

- 4 x 125g (4 ounces) baby orange sweet potato, halved lengthways
- 1 tablespoon olive oil
- 2 teaspoons ground allspice
- 1 tablespoon sumac
- ¼ cup (40g) sesame seeds
- ¼ cup (60ml) olive oil, extra
- 1 tablespoon lemon juice
- 12 french-trimmed lamb cutlets (600g)
- 2 cups (500ml) water
- 1 cup (200g) white quinoa, rinsed
- 1 teaspoon ground turmeric
- 2 tablespoons chopped fresh flat-leaf parsley
- 2 tablespoons flat-leaf parsley leaves, extra

RAITA
- 1 lebanese cucumber (130g), grated coarsely
- ⅔ cup (190g) Greek-style yoghurt
- 1 clove garlic, crushed
- 2 tablespoons shredded fresh mint leaves

1 Preheat oven to 200°C/400°F. Oil an oven tray then line with baking paper.

2 Place sweet potato on tray; drizzle with oil. Roast for 40 minutes or until soft. Cover to keep warm. Gently squash.

3 Meanwhile, combine allspice, sumac, sesame seeds, 1 tablespoon of the extra oil and the juice in a shallow dish; season. Add cutlets; turn to coat in mixture.

4 Bring the water to the boil in a medium saucepan; add quinoa and turmeric, return to the boil. Reduce heat to medium-low; simmer, uncovered, for 10 minutes or until quinoa is tender. Drain well. Return quinoa to same pan with remaining extra oil and chopped parsley; stir to combine. Season to taste.

5 Make raita.

6 Cook cutlets on a heated oiled barbecue (or grill plate or grill) for 5 minutes each side or until browned both sides and cooked as desired. Cover, rest for 5 minutes.

7 Serve cutlets with quinoa, sweet potato and raita. Sprinkle with extra parsley.

raita Squeeze grated cucumber to remove excess liquid. Combine cucumber with remaining ingredients in a small bowl. Season to taste.

TIPS

You can use 12 lamb loin chops for a more economical version. The tumeric quinoa and raita can be made several hours ahead.

Giant meatballs
ON CREAMY POLENTA

PREP + COOK TIME 45 MINUTES **SERVES** 4

- 500g (1 pound) minced (ground) beef
- 1 medium brown onion (150g), grated coarsely
- 1 medium zucchini (120g), grated coarsely
- 1 medium carrot (120g), grated finely
- 1 egg
- 1 tablespoon dijon mustard
- 1 tablespoon chopped fresh rosemary leaves
- 1 cup (70g) gluten-free breadcrumbs
- 2 tablespoons olive oil
- 1 litre (4 cups) passata
- 1 clove garlic, crushed
- 1 tablespoon balsamic vinegar
- 1 teaspoon brown sugar
- ½ cup (125ml) water
- ½ cup firmly packed fresh small basil leaves

POLENTA

- 1 litre (4 cups) water
- 1 cup (170g) instant polenta (cornmeal)
- 40g (1½ ounces) butter, chopped
- ½ cup (40g) finely grated parmesan

1 Combine beef, onion, zucchini, carrot, egg, mustard, rosemary and breadcrumbs in a large bowl; season well. Roll mixture into 16 balls.

2 Heat half the oil in a large frying pan over a medium heat; cook meatballs, in batches, for 5 minutes or until browned all over, adding remaining oil as necessary. Drain meatballs on paper towel.

3 Add passata to same cleaned pan with garlic, vinegar, sugar and the water; bring to the boil. Return meatballs to pan; toss to coat in sauce. Reduce heat to low; simmer, covered, for 15 minutes or until meatballs are cooked through and sauce is thickened slightly.

4 Meanwhile, make polenta.

5 Serve meatballs and sauce on polenta; top with basil.

polenta Bring the water to the boil in a medium saucepan. Gradually add polenta, stirring, constantly. Reduce heat to low; cook, stirring, for 5 minutes or until the polenta is soft and creamy. Stir in butter and parmesan; season to taste. Cover to keep warm.

If polenta thickens on standing, add a little milk, water or stock until it reaches the desired consistency.

NUTRITIONAL COUNT PER SERVING
23.5g total fat
6.3g saturated fat
2511kJ (601 cal)
61.3g carbohydrate
33.2g protein
4.8g fibre

Plus

DAIRY FREE
YEAST FREE
EGG FREE

Crisp green bean
& PORK STIR-FRY

PREP + COOK TIME 30 MINUTES · **SERVES 4**

- 1⅓ cups (265g) jasmine rice
- 2 cups (500ml) water
- 2 tablespoons peanut oil
- 300g (9½ ounces) green beans, cut into 5cm (2-inch) lengths
- 500g (1 pound) minced (ground) pork
- 3 green onions (scallions), sliced
- 1 tablespoon grated fresh ginger
- 2 cloves garlic, chopped
- 1 tablespoon finely chopped fresh coriander (cilantro) stems
- ¼ cup (60ml) gluten-free hoisin sauce
- 1 tablespoon tamari
- 1 teaspoon sesame oil
- ⅓ cup fresh coriander (cilantro) leaves

1 Rinse rice under cold running water until liquid runs clear; drain well. Add rice to a medium saucepan with the water, cover; bring to the boil. Reduce heat to low; cook, covered, for 10 minutes or until rice is tender. Stand covered.

2 Meanwhile, heat half the peanut oil in a wok or large frying pan over high heat; stir-fry beans, in batches, until the skin begins to blister. Remove from wok.

3 Add remaining peanut oil to wok over a high heat; stir-fry pork for 5 minutes or until browned.

4 Add green onion, ginger, garlic and coriander stems; stir-fry for 1 minute. Add hoisin, tamari and sesame oil; stir-fry until heated through. Return beans to wok; toss to combine.

5 Top stir-fry with coriander leaves; serve with rice.

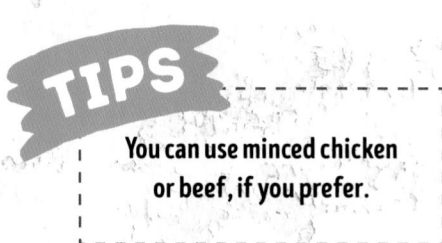

TIPS

You can use minced chicken or beef, if you prefer.

Bibimbap

PREP + COOK TIME 50 MINUTES (+ STANDING) SERVES 4

- 400g (12½ ounces) beef rump steak, trimmed, sliced thinly
- 2 tablespoons tamari
- 1 tablespoon finely grated fresh ginger
- 1 clove garlic, chopped
- 2 teaspoons sesame oil
- 2 cups (400g) short-grain white sushi rice
- 2 cups (500ml) water
- 8 dried shiitake mushrooms (20g)
- 150g (4½ ounces) baby spinach leaves
- 2 cups (160g) bean sprouts, trimmed
- 2 tablespoons sesame oil, extra
- 2 tablespoons vegetable oil
- 1 large carrot (180g), cut into matchsticks
- 4 eggs
- ⅓ cup (85g) kimchi (see tips)
- 1 tablespoon hot chilli sauce

TIPS

Kimchi is a traditional Korean side dish of fermented vegetables with a variety of seasonings.

1 Combine beef, tamari, ginger, garlic and sesame oil in a medium bowl. Stand for 20 minutes.

2 Meanwhile, rinse rice under cold running water until water runs clear; drain well. Add rice to medium saucepan with the water. Cover; bring to the boil. Reduce heat to low; cook, covered, for 15 minutes or until tender. Stand covered until required.

3 Place mushrooms in a small heatproof bowl; cover with boiling water. Stand for 15 minutes; drain. Discard stems from mushrooms; slice mushroom caps thinly.

4 Boil, steam or microwave spinach and sprouts, separately, until tender; drain, cool slightly. Squeeze excess liquid from spinach. Place spinach and sprouts in separate small bowls, add 2 teaspoons of the extra sesame oil to each; season with salt.

5 Heat 2 teaspoons of the extra sesame oil and the vegetable oil in a medium frying pan over medium heat; cook carrot, stirring for 2 minutes or until carrot is just tender. Remove from pan.

6 Cook beef in same pan over high heat, in batches, stirring, for 5 minutes or until beef is browned and tender.

7 Wipe out pan. Heat remaining sesame oil in pan over medium heat; fry eggs for 3 minutes or until eggs are cooked to your liking.

8 Arrange beef and vegetables on rice; top with eggs. Serve with kimchi and chilli sauce.

**NUTRITIONAL
COUNT PER SERVING**
31g total fat
6.5g saturated fat
3344kJ (800 cal)
88.2g carbohydrate
37g protein
3.5g fibre

Cauliflower pizza with
TOMATOES & SALAMI

PREP + COOK TIME 45 MINUTES **SERVES** 4

- 700g (1½ pounds) cauliflower florets
- 1 egg
- ½ cup (40g) grated parmesan
- 1 teaspoon dried oregano
- ¼ cup (60ml) passata
- 2 teaspoons tomato paste
- 1 tablespoon shredded fresh basil
- 150g (4½ ounces) baby bocconcini, torn
- 50g (1½ ounces) sliced gluten-free salami
- 100g (3 ounces) mixed baby tomatoes, halved
- ⅓ cup (55g) kalamata olives
- 1 tablespoon drained capers
- 1 tablespoon fresh baby basil leaves, extra

1 Preheat oven to 220°C/425°F. Line a 30cm (12-inch) round pizza tray with baking paper. Place a pizza stone in the oven while oven is preheating.

2 Process or blend cauliflower until finely chopped. Boil, steam or microwave cauliflower until soft; cool slightly. Place cauliflower into a clean tea towel; squeeze to remove excess moisture. Place cauliflower in a medium bowl with egg, parmesan and oregano; season. Mix well with your hands until combined. Press cauliflower mixture firmly on pizza tray.

3 Bake on pizza stone for 15 minutes or until crisp and golden. Increase oven to 230°C/450°F.

4 Combine passata, paste and basil in a small bowl. Spread over pizza base, leaving a 2cm (¾-inch) border. Top with bocconcini, salami, tomatoes, olives and capers.

5 Bake for a further 10 minutes or until bocconcini has melted and is golden. Top with extra basil leaves to serve.

TIPS

Don't have too much overhang as the paper will burn at high temperatures. If you don't have a pizza stone, heat oven to hottest temperature using the base element and fan-forced if you have the option. Otherwise, use fan-forced only. Cook on the lowest shelf in the oven to help the base to crisp.

Baked chermoulla fish
WITH TOMATO POTATO BAKE

PREP + COOK TIME 1¼ HOURS SERVES 4

- 5 medium potatoes (1kg), sliced thinly
- 1 large red onion (300g), sliced thinly
- 1 tablespoon fresh rosemary sprigs
- 3 medium ripe tomatoes (450g), sliced
- 2 cups (500ml) gluten-free chicken stock
- 1 tablespoon olive oil
- 2 x 800g (1½-pound) whole snapper, cleaned
- 1 medium lemon (140g), sliced

CHERMOULLA

- 1 cup loosely packed fresh flat-leaf parsley
- 1 cup loosely packed fresh coriander (cilantro) leaves
- 1 small brown onion (80g), chopped
- 1 clove garlic, chopped
- 1 tablespoon sweet paprika
- 1 tablespoon ground cumin
- 2 tablespoons lemon juice
- 2 tablespoons extra virgin olive oil

1 Preheat oven to 200°C/400°F. Oil a 20cm x 30cm (8-inch x 12-inch) rectangular ovenproof dish.

2 Layer potato, onion, rosemary and tomato in dish. Pour stock over potatoes; cover. Bake, covered, for 40 minutes. Remove cover, brush top with oil; bake, uncovered, for a further 30 minutes or until potato is soft and golden.

3 Meanwhile, make chermoulla.

4 Line a shallow oven dish with baking paper. Score fish twice through the thickest part on both sides. Fill the cavity and slits with lemon slices. Rub chermoulla over both sides of fish. Place fish in lined dish.

5 Place fish in oven, alongside potato, for last 25 minutes of potato cooking time or until fish is cooked.

6 Serve fish with potato bake, topped with coriander sprigs, if you like.

chermoulla Process ingredients until smooth; season.

TIPS

We used snapper in this recipe, but any large white fish would be fine. The fish and potato are delicious cooked in a covered barbecue as it imparts a wonderful smoky flavour. The fish can be added to the barbecue if space permits when you uncover the potato.

Plus
NUT FREE
DAIRY FREE
YEAST FREE
EGG FREE

NUTRITIONAL
COUNT PER SERVING
18g total fat
3.4g saturated fat
2194kJ (525 cal)
33.7g carbohydrate
50g protein
9.8g fibre

**NUTRITIONAL
COUNT PER SERVING**
28.1g total fat
5.9g saturated fat
2130kJ (510 cal)
37.3g carbohydrate
25.8g protein
1.6g fibre

Japanese pork &
VEGETABLE PANCAKES

PREP + COOK TIME 40 MINUTES SERVES 4

You will need ½ small white sweet potato for this recipe.

- 4 eggs
- 1 cup (135g) gluten-free plain (all-purpose) flour
- ½ cup (125ml) water
- ½ cup (60g) coarsely grated white sweet potato
- 2 tablespoons peanut oil
- 300g (9½ ounces) pork fillet, sliced thinly
- 2 cups (90g) finely shredded wombok (napa cabbage)
- 2 green onions (scallions), sliced thinly
- 2 tablespoons drained pickled ginger
- 2 tablespoons gluten-free worcestershire sauce
- 2 tablespoons tomato sauce (ketchup)
- 2 tablespoons japanese mayonnaise
- 2 green onions (scallions), extra, sliced thinly

1 Whisk eggs, flour and the water in a large bowl until smooth. Stir in sweet potato; season.

2 Heat half the oil in a large frying pan over medium heat; stir-fry pork, in batches, for 5 minutes or until browned and tender. Remove from pan.

3 Pour ½ cup of the batter into same pan; top with a quarter of the pork, cabbage, onion and ginger. Cook over medium-low heat for 3 minutes or until the base is golden and set. Turn over; cook until browned lightly. Remove from pan; cover to keep warm. Repeat with remaining batter, pork, cabbage, onion and ginger to make four pancakes in total.

4 Brush top of pancakes with combined sauces; drizzle with mayonnaise (see tips). Serve topped with extra green onions.

TIPS

To drizzle mayonnaise place in a snap-lock bag, cut a small opening in corner. Pancakes are best made close to serving. Gluten-free worcestershire sauce is available from some health food stores. Plunge extra green onions in a bowl of iced water and stand for 15 minutes or until curled, if you like.

Chunky minestrone with
HALOUMI & PESTO VERDE

PREP + COOK TIME 1½ HOURS (+ STANDING) **SERVES** 6

You will need to start this recipe a day ahead.

- ½ cup (100g) dried red kidney beans
- ¼ cup (50g) buckwheat
- 2 tablespoons olive oil
- 2 baby leeks (250g), sliced thinly
- 150g (6½ ounces) pancetta, chopped
- 1 large carrot (180g), chopped
- 2 stalks trimmed celery (200g), chopped
- 1 small orange sweet potato (250g), chopped
- 2 large zucchini (300g), chopped
- 2 medium parsnips (500g), chopped
- 800g (1½ pounds) canned chopped tomatoes
- 1 litre (4 cups) gluten-free chicken or vegetable stock
- 2 cups (500ml) water
- 1 bay leaf
- 250g (8 ounces) haloumi, sliced thickly

PESTO VERDE

- 2 cups coarsely chopped fresh flat-leaf parsley
- ⅓ cup (65g) drained capers, chopped
- 1 teaspoon finely grated lemon rind
- 2 tablespoons lemon juice
- ⅓ cup (40g) finely grated parmesan
- ¼ cup (60ml) extra virgin olive oil

1 Place beans and buckwheat in separate medium bowls with enough cold water to cover; stand overnight. Drain beans and buckwheat separately, rinse under cold water.

2 Place beans in a medium saucepan of boiling water. Return to the boil; simmer, uncovered, for 20 minutes or until beans are just tender. Drain.

3 Heat half the oil in a large saucepan over medium heat; cook leek and pancetta, stirring, for 10 minutes or until leek is soft. Add carrot and celery; cook, stirring, for 5 minutes. Add sweet potato, zucchini, parsnip, tomatoes, stock, water and bay leaf; bring to the boil. Reduce heat to low; simmer, covered, for 30 minutes.

4 Stir in buckwheat; simmer, covered, for 15 minutes or until buckwheat is tender. Add beans to soup; cook, uncovered for 5 minutes or until hot. Season.

5 Meanwhile, make pesto verde.

6 Heat remaining oil in a medium frying pan over medium heat; cook haloumi, in batches, until browned on both sides.

7 Serve soup topped with haloumi and pesto verde.

pesto verde Blend or process ingredients until well combined. Season.

TIPS

Soup can be made up to 3 days ahead; keep covered in the refrigerator. Soup can be frozen for up to 3 months. Pesto verde can be made a day ahead; keep tightly covered in the fridge or it can be frozen in a small container for up to 3 months.

NUTRITIONAL COUNT PER SERVING
35.7g total fat
11.2g saturated fat
2541kJ (608 cal)
30.3g carbohydrate
34.5g protein
12.4g fibre

Plus

**YEAST FREE
NUT FREE**

NUTRITIONAL COUNT PER SERVING
25.8g total fat
16.4g saturated fat
2041kJ (488 cal)
27.6g carbohydrate
33.4g protein
6.6g fibre

Plus
**NUT FREE
DAIRY FREE
YEAST FREE
EGG FREE**

Lemon grass & coconut soup
WITH CHICKEN DUMPLINGS

PREP + COOK TIME 1 HOUR SERVES 4

- 4 stalks fresh lemon grass, chopped coarsely
- 10cm (4-inch) piece fresh galangal or ginger (50g), peeled, sliced
- 8 red asian shallots (200g), chopped coarsely
- 3 cloves garlic, sliced
- 800ml canned light coconut milk
- 2 cups (500ml) gluten-free chicken stock
- 2 tablespoons fish sauce
- 8 kaffir lime leaves, torn
- 1 cup (250ml) water
- 100g (3 ounces) small button mushrooms, sliced
- 500g (1 pound) minced (ground) chicken
- ½ cup (100g) jasmine rice
- 170g (5½ ounces) broccolini, trimmed, cut into thirds
- 150g (4½ ounces) green beans, sliced thinly lengthways
- 1 cup (80g) bean sprouts, trimmed
- 2 tablespoons chopped fresh coriander (cilantro) leaves
- 1 fresh long red chilli, seeded, sliced thinly
- lime wedges, to serve

1 Pound lemon grass and galangal with a mortar and pestle until crushed coarsely. Transfer to a large saucepan; add shallots, garlic, coconut milk, stock and sauce. Bring to the boil. Reduce heat to low; simmer, covered, for 20 minutes.

2 Strain broth through a fine sieve into another large saucepan; discard solids. Add lime leaves and water; bring to the boil. Add mushrooms, reduce heat to low; cook, covered, for 10 minutes or until mushrooms are just tender.

3 Meanwhile, roll chicken into 16 small balls. Drop chicken dumplings into soup, then add rice. Simmer, uncovered, for 10 minutes or until chicken is cooked through and rice is just tender, stirring occasionally.

4 Add broccolini and beans to soup; simmer, covered, for 3 minutes or until vegetables are just tender. Season.

5 Ladle soup into bowls, divide sprouts between bowls. Top with coriander and chilli, season with cracked pepper. Serve with lime wedges.

TIPS

You can use minced (ground) pork instead of chicken. The soup can be made to the end of step 2 up to 2 days ahead; cover and keep in the fridge. The balls can be made and kept on a tray, covered, in the fridge for up to 1 day.

Zucchini pasta
WITH AVOCADO PESTO

PREP + COOK TIME 40 MINUTES **SERVES 4**

- 8 large zucchini (1.2kg)
- 2 cups firmly packed fresh basil leaves
- 2 cloves garlic, chopped
- ¼ cup (40g) pine nuts, toasted
- ½ cup (40g) finely grated parmesan
- 1 tablespoon extra virgin olive oil
- 1 medium avocado (250g), chopped
- 50g (1½ ounces) baby rocket (arugula) leaves
- 1 teaspoon finely grated lemon rind
- 2 tablespoons lemon juice
- 2 tablespoons finely grated parmesan, extra
- 2 tablespoons pine nuts, toasted, extra
- 2 tablespoons fresh baby basil leaves, extra

1 Using a vegetable spiralizer, cut zucchini into thick noodles. Place the zucchini in a large steamer or colander over a large pan of simmering water, ensuring the base of the steamer is not touching the water. Cover; steam for 2 minutes or until the zucchini is just tender (do not overcook or it will fall apart).

2 Blend or process basil, garlic, pine nuts, parmesan and oil until smooth. Add avocado; process until smooth. Season.

3 Toss zucchini with half the avocado pesto. Serve zucchini pasta topped with rocket, rind, juice, extra parmesan, remaining pesto, extra pine nuts and extra basil leaves.

TIPS

You will need a spiralizer for this recipe; they can be purchased at kitchenware stores.

Plus
**YEAST FREE
EGG FREE**

**NUTRITIONAL
COUNT PER SERVING**
33.1g total fat
7g saturated fat
1577kJ (377 cal)
6.1g carbohydrate
11.7g protein
6.2g fibre

Chia-crusted salmon
WITH CORN SALAD

PREP + COOK TIME 40 MINUTES **SERVES** 4

- 2 trimmed cobs corn (500g)
- 300g (9½ ounces) kale, stalks removed
- 1 medium red capsicum (bell pepper) (200g), chopped finely
- 2 green onions (scallions), sliced
- 2 tablespoons chopped fresh dill
- 2 tablespoons pepitas (pumpkin seed kernels)
- 1 tablespoons dijon mustard
- 1 tablespoon apple cider vinegar
- 1 teaspoon honey
- ⅓ cup (80ml) extra virgin olive oil
- 4 x 160g (5-ounce) salmon fillets, skin on
- 2 tablespoons black chia seeds
- 1 lime (90g), cut into wedges

1 Boil, steam or microwave corn until tender; cool slightly. Cut kernels from cob.

2 Meanwhile, place kale in a heatproof bowl; cover with boiling water, stand for 2 minutes or until bright green. Drain; rinse kale under cold water. Tear into pieces.

3 Combine corn kernels, kale, capsicum, onion, dill and pepitas in a large bowl.

4 Whisk mustard, vinegar, honey and 2 tablespoons of the oil in a small bowl. Pour dressing over corn mixture; season, toss gently to combine.

5 Pat salmon dry with paper towel. Place chia seeds on a plate; press salmon flesh-side down onto seeds to coat.

6 Heat remaining oil in a large frying pan over a medium heat; cook salmon, chia-side down, for 5 minutes or until crisp and golden. Turn salmon; cook skin-side down until skin is crisp and salmon is cooked to your liking.

7 Serve salmon with corn salad and lime wedges.

TIPS

Swap black chia seeds for white chia seeds.

Lamb & buckwheat kofta
WITH EGG SALAD

PREP + COOK TIME 50 MINUTES (+ REFRIGERATION) **SERVES** 4

- ¼ cup (50g) buckwheat
- 300g (9½ ounces) minced (ground) lamb
- 200g (6½ ounces) minced (ground) beef
- 1 teaspoon ground cinnamon
- 1 teaspoon ground allspice
- 1 teaspoon ground black pepper
- 1 medium brown onion (150g), grated coarsely
- 2 cloves garlic, crushed
- 4 eggs
- 1 medium eggplant (300g), sliced thinly lengthways
- ¼ cup (60ml) olive oil
- 100g (3 ounces) mixed salad leaves
- 2 tablespoons chopped fresh flat-leaf parsley leaves
- ⅓ cup (70g) Greek-style yoghurt
- 1 teaspoon ground sumac
- 1 tablespoon pomegranate molasses
- 1 medium pomegranate (320g), seeds removed (see tips)

1 Cook buckwheat in small saucepan of boiling water for 15 minutes or until just tender. Drain; rinse under cold water, drain well.

2 Combine buckwheat, lamb, beef, spices, onion and garlic in a large bowl; season well. Shape heaped tablespoons of mixture into ovals; place on a tray. Cover; refrigerate for 30 minutes.

3 Meanwhile, place eggs in a small saucepan, cover with cold water. Bring to the boil; boil for 6 minutes; drain. Cut in half.

4 Toss eggplant in 2 tablespoons of the oil to coat. Cook eggplant, on a heated grill plate or barbecue over medium-high heat for 5 minutes or until browned on both sides and cooked through. Cover to keep warm.

5 Brush remaining oil over kofta. Cook kofta on a heated grill plate for 8 minutes or until browned all over and cooked through.

6 Serve kofta on combined salad leaves and parsley, with eggplant and eggs. Drizzle with yoghurt and with pomegranate molasses; sprinkle with pomegranate seeds. Season to taste.

TIPS

To remove seeds from pomegranate, cut in half crossways; hold it, cut-side down, in the palm of your hand over a bowl, then hit the outside firmly with a wooden spoon. The seeds should fall out easily; discard any white pith that falls out with them. Kofta can be prepared a day ahead; keep covered in the fridge. Kofta can be frozen in a container for up to 3 months.

Plus
**YEAST FREE
NUT FREE**

Plain DHAL

PREP + COOK TIME 50 MINUTES SERVES 4

- 1½ cups (300g) moong dal or red lentils
- 1 teaspoon turmeric
- 1 teaspoon garam masala
- 1 teaspoon mustard seeds
- 1 tablespoon finely grated fresh ginger
- 1 dried red chilli
- 6 fresh curry leaves
- 1 teaspoon salt
- 1 tablespoon ghee
- 1 litres (4 cups) water
- 1 tablespoon ghee, extra
- 1 tablespoon lemon juice

CUMIN & CHILLI ROTI

- 1 teaspoon cumin seeds
- ½ teaspoon chilli flakes
- 1 cup (150g) chickpea (besan) flour
- ¼ teaspoon xanthan gum
- 2 tablespoons buttermilk
- 2 tablesppoons water
- 1 tablespoon vegetable oil
- chickpea (besan) flour, extra, for dusting
- 2 tablespoons ghee

1 Make cumin and chilli roti.

2 Rinse moong dal under cold water until liquid runs clear; drain.

3 Add moong dal, spices, ginger, chilli, leaves, salt, ghee and the water to a medium saucepan, stir to combine. Bring to the boil. Reduce heat to low; simmer, uncovered, for 20 minutes or until dhal is just tender.

4 Stir in extra ghee and the juice; season.

cumin & chilli roti Stir cumin and chilli in a small dry frying pan, over medium heat, for 1 minute or until fragrant. Combine spices with chickpea flour and xanthan gum in a large bowl; season. Add buttermilk, the water and oil; stir to form a firm dough. Divide dough into eight balls. Flour work surface with extra chickpea flour; roll out each ball into 2mm (⅛-inch) thick, 12cm (4¾-inch) rounds. Brush a heated small frying pan with ghee; cook roti, over high heat, for 1 minute each side or until lightly golden and cooked through. Transfer to a plate, cover with foil to keep warm. Repeat with roti dough and ghee.

TIPS

Moong dal are dried mung beans, available from Indian grocers and some health food stores.

4 ways with PLAIN DHAL

NUTRITIONAL COUNT PER SERVING WITH ROTI
34g total fat
17.9g saturated fat
2646kJ (633 cal)
48.9g carbohydrate
27.1g protein
15.6g fibre

Plus
**NUT FREE
YEAST FREE
EGG FREE**

Plus
**NUT FREE
YEAST FREE
EGG FREE**

NUTRITIONAL COUNT PER SERVING WITH ROTI
28.5g total fat
14.1g saturated fat
2568kJ (614 cal)
55.6g carbohydrate
27.5g protein
16.8g fibre

SWEET POTATO & CARROT DHAL

PREP + COOK TIME 30 MINUTES SERVES 4

Make plain dhal using recipe on page 169, adding 1½ cups (185g) coarsely grated orange sweet potato and ½ cup (120g) coarsely grated carrot to step 3. Season. Serve dhal with cumin and chilli roti on page 169, topped with yoghurt, if you like.

COCONUT, KALE & ZUCCHINI DHAL

PREP + COOK TIME 35 MINUTES SERVES 4

Make plain dhal using recipe on page 169, adding 1½ cups (185g) coarsely grated zucchini to step 3. Stir in 1 cup (45g) firmly packed finely shredded kale leaves and ¼ cup (60ml) light coconut cream; cook for 3 minutes or until the kale wilts. Stir in 20g (¾oz) ghee and 1 tablespoon lemon juice, just before serving. Season. Serve dhal with cumin and chilli roti on page 169, and lemon wedges, if you like.

Tip You will need 2 medium zucchini (240g) for this recipe.

Plus
NUT FREE
YEAST FREE
EGG FREE

NUTRITIONAL COUNT PER SERVING WITH ROTI
39.2g total fat
(21g saturated fat)
2867kJ (686 cal)
50g carbohydrate
27.7g protein
15.8g fibre

NUTRITIONAL COUNT PER SERVING WITH ROTI
28.5g total fat
14.1g saturated fat
2610kJ (624 cal)
57.1g carbohydrate
28.3g protein
16.1g fibre

Plus
NUT FREE
YEAST FREE
EGG FREE

TOMATO, GINGER & CORIANDER DHAL

PREP + COOK TIME 30 MINUTES SERVES 4

Make plain dhal using recipe on page 169, adding 250g (8oz) halved cherry tomatoes and ½ cup light cream to step 3. Stir in 20g (¾oz) ghee, just before serving. Season. Serve dhal with cumin and chilli roti on page 169, topped with coriander leaves, if you like.

CURRIED SPINACH & POTATO DHAL

PREP + COOK TIME 35 MINUTES SERVES 4

Make plain dhal using recipe on page 169, adding 2 diced medium (400g) potatoes to step 3. Stir in 75g (2½oz) baby spinach leaves; cover; stand for 5 minutes or until spinach wilts. Stir in 20g (¾oz) ghee and 1 tablespoon lemon juice, just before serving. Season. Serve dhal with cumin and chilli roti on page 169.

Vegetable lasagne with
CAULIFLOWER RICOTTA SAUCE

PREP + COOK TIME 2 HOURS **SERVES** 6

- 1kg (2 pounds) jap pumpkin, cut into thick wedges
- 5 large zucchini (750g), sliced thickly lengthways
- ½ small cauliflower (500g), cut into small florets
- ¼ cup (60ml) olive oil
- 1 large brown onion (200g), chopped
- 3 trimmed stalks celery (300g), chopped
- 1 large carrot (180g), chopped
- ½ cup (125ml) white wine
- 800g (1½ pounds) canned chopped tomatoes
- 1 bay leaf
- 2 tablespoons chopped fresh basil leaves
- 2 tablespoons chopped fresh thyme leaves
- 2 tablespoons chopped fresh oregano leaves
- 270g (8½ ounces) bottled chargrilled red capsicum (bell peppers), drained, sliced
- 1 cup (250ml) water
- 500g (1 pound) ricotta
- ¾ cup (180ml) milk
- 1 cup (80g) grated parmesan
- 280g (9 ounces) gluten-free fresh lasagne sheets

1 Preheat oven to 200°C/400°F. Line three oven trays with baking paper.

2 Place pumpkin, zucchini and cauliflower on separate oven trays. Drizzle with 1½ tablespoons of the oil; season with sea salt.

3 Roast pumpkin for 10 minutes. Add zucchini and cauliflower; roast for a further 30 minutes or until vegetables are tender. Reserve four slices of zucchini for the top. Reduce oven to 180°C/350°F.

4 Heat remaining oil in a large deep frying pan over medium heat; cook onion, celery and carrot, stirring, for 10 minutes or until soft. Add wine; bring to the boil. Boil for 5 minutes or until most of the wine is evaporated.

5 Stir in tomatoes, herbs, capsicum and the water; bring to the boil. Reduce heat; simmer, covered, for 20 minutes or until thickened slightly. Season to taste.

6 Process cauliflower until smooth. Transfer to a medium bowl; stir in ricotta, milk and ¾ cup of the parmesan. Season to taste.

7 Spoon 2 tablespoons of the tomato mixture over base of a 20cm x 30cm (8-inch x 12-inch) ovenproof dish. Top with a layer of lasagne sheets, then a layer of pumpkin, zucchini and cauliflower mixture. Repeat with remaining ingredients, finishing with a layer of cauliflower mixture then reserved zucchini. Sprinkle with remaining parmesan.

8 Bake for 45 minutes or until lasagne sheets are tender. Serve topped with extra basil leaves, if you like.

TIPS

To evenly roast the vegetables, rotate oven trays during cooking in non-fan forced ovens. You can remove the skin from the pumpkin if you prefer. Lasagne can be made several hours ahead.

Plus

**YEAST FREE
NUT FREE**

**NUTRITIONAL
COUNT PER SERVING**
28.1g total fat
10.8g saturated fat
2550kJ (610 cal)
51.9g carbohydrate
25.6g protein
14.8g fibre

**NUTRITIONAL
COUNT PER SERVING**
42.7g total fat
15.5g saturated fat
2591kJ (620 cal)
12.3g carbohydrate
41.7g protein
9.3g fibre

Slow-cooked lamb with
GARLICKY BROAD BEANS

PREP + COOK TIME 4½ HOURS (+ REFRIGERATION & STANDING) **SERVES 8**

- 1 cup (280g) Greek-style yoghurt
- 2 cloves garlic, sliced
- 1 teaspoon ground turmeric
- 1 tablespoon ground cumin
- 1 tablespoon sweet paprika
- 1.5kg (3-pound) boneless lamb shoulder
- ⅓ cup (80ml) olive oil
- 1 large brown onion (200g), chopped finely
- 2 cloves garlic, crushed, extra
- 2 large potatoes (600g), cut into 2cm (¾-inch) cubes
- 1kg (2 pounds) frozen broad (fava) beans, thawed, peeled
- 1 medium lemon (140g), cut into wedges

1 Combine yoghurt, garlic and spices in a large bowl. Add lamb; rub yoghurt mixture over lamb, season. Cover, refrigerate for 3 hours or overnight.

2 Preheat oven to 160°C/325°F.

3 Wrap lamb in foil to enclose; place on an oven tray. Bake for 4 hours or until lamb is tender and falling apart. Stand for 15 minutes.

4 Meanwhile, heat oil in a large frying pan over medium-low heat; cook onion, stirring occasionally, for 7 minutes or until soft but not coloured. Add extra garlic; cook, stirring, for 2 minutes. Add potato; cook, covered, for 15 minutes, stirring occasionally, until potatoes are just tender.

5 Add broad beans; cook, covered, for 5 minutes or until the beans and potato are soft. Season.

6 Serve broad bean mixture topped with shredded lamb, pan juices and with lemon wedges.

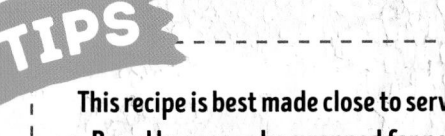

TIPS

This recipe is best made close to serving.
Broad beans can be swapped for peas.

SWEETS

Lemontons

PREP + COOK TIME 1 HOUR (+ STANDING) MAKES 16

- 4 eggs
- ⅔ cup (150g) caster (superfine) sugar
- ⅓ cup (50g) 100% corn (maize) cornflour (cornstarch)
- ⅓ cup (45g) gluten-free self-raising flour
- ⅓ cup (45g) gluten-free plain (all-purpose) flour
- 3 cups (300g) shredded coconut

LEMON ICING

- 1 cup (250ml) store-bought gluten-free lemon curd
- 1½ cups (240g) gluten-free icing (confectioners') sugar
- ⅓ cup (80ml) lemon juice
- ½ cup (125ml) boiling water

TIPS

Lemontons can be made a day ahead;
store in an airtight container.

1 Preheat oven to 180°C/350°F. Grease a deep 23cm (9-inch) square cake pan; line base with baking paper.

2 Beat eggs and caster sugar in a large bowl with an electric mixer for 8 minutes or until mixture is thick and creamy.

3 Triple sift flours. Whisk flour mixture into egg mixture until just combined. Pour mixture into pan.

4 Bake cake for 25 minutes or until cake is dry to the touch and edges are coming away from the sides of the pan. Stand cake in pan for 5 minutes before turning, top-side up, onto a wire rack to cool completely.

5 Meanwhile, make lemon icing.

6 Cut cake into 16 squares. Use two forks to dip squares, one at a time, into lemon icing until coated all over; toss in coconut. Place on a wire rack until firm.

lemon icing Whisk lemon curd, sifted icing sugar, juice and the water in a large bowl until well combined.

variations

strawberry Dip the sponge into gluten-free strawberry topping and coat in coconut tinted with pink food colouring.

chocolate Replace lemon icing with combined 4 cups (460g) gluten-free icing (confectioners') sugar, ½ cup (50g) sifted cocoa powder, 15g (½ ounce) melted butter and 1 cup (250ml) milk in a medium heatproof bowl, over a pan of simmering water; stir until icing is of a coating consistency.

white chocolate Replace lemon icing with combined 4 cups (460g) gluten-free icing (confectioners') sugar and ¾ cup (180ml) milk in a medium heatproof bowl, over a pan of simmering water; stir until icing is of a coating consistency. Add 100g finely grated white chocolate to coconut.

NUTRITIONAL COUNT PER LEMONTON
16.5g total fat
11.1g saturated fat
1239kJ (296 cal)
41.8g carbohydrate
3.6g protein
2.9g fibre

Plus
YEAST FREE NUT FREE

NUTRITIONAL
COUNT PER SERVING
24.7g total fat
13.6g saturated fat
1838kJ (440 cal)
46.7g carbohydrate
6.3g protein
5.6g fibre

Plus
**DAIRY FREE
YEAST FREE
EGG FREE**

Raspberry ripple
SWEETCORN ICE-CREAM

PREP + COOK TIME 1½ HOURS (+ STANDING & FREEZING) **MAKES** 1 LITRE (SERVES 8)

This healthy non-dairy ice-cream is made with corn, which provides a natural creaminess and sweetness. Expect the ice-cream to be slightly more icy as a result.

- 2 trimmed corn cobs (500g)
- 2¼ cups (560ml) coconut cream
- 2 cups (500ml) unsweetened almond milk
- ¼ cup (55g) caster (superfine) sugar
- 2 teaspoons vanilla extract
- ½ cup (125ml) agave syrup
- 1½ cups (225g) fresh or thawed frozen raspberries

CORNFLAKE CRUNCH

- 2 tablespoons caster (superfine) sugar
- 1 tablespoon agave syrup
- 1 tablespoon olive oil
- ½ teaspoon vanilla extract
- 2 cups (80g) gluten-free cornflakes

TIPS

Take the ice-cream out of the freezer 15 to 30 minutes before serving to soften it slightly. You could freeze the ice-cream mixture into blocks or popsicle moulds and roll in cornflake crunch before serving.

1 Using a sharp knife, cut kernels from cobs; reserve cobs. Place corn kernels, cobs, coconut cream, almond milk and sugar in a large saucepan over medium-high heat; bring to the boil. Reduce heat; simmer for 5 minutes or until corn is tender. Stand for 1 hour.

2 Discard corn cobs. Blend or process corn mixture until smooth. Strain corn mixture; discard solids. Stir in vanilla and ⅓ cup of the agave syrup until combined. Refrigerate until cold.

3 Transfer corn mixture to an ice-cream machine. Churn mixture following manufacturer's instructions.

4 Meanwhile, blend or process raspberries with remaining agave syrup until smooth. Swirl raspberry mixture through almost frozen ice-cream to create a ripple effect; pour into a 1 litre (4-cup) freezer-proof container. Freeze overnight or until firm.

5 Make cornflake crunch.

6 Serve ice-cream topped with cornflake crunch.

cornflake crunch Preheat oven to 150°C/300°F. Line an oven tray with baking paper. Place sugar, agave syrup, oil and vanilla in a small saucepan over low heat, stirring, until sugar dissolves. Place cornflakes in a medium bowl. Add syrup mixture; stir to combine. Spread cornflake mixture on tray. Bake for 25 minutes or until slightly more golden. Leave to cool. Break into small pieces.

Glazed fig & whole
ORANGE CAKES

PREP + COOK TIME 3 HOURS 20 MINUTES (+ STANDING) **MAKES** 12

- 6 dried figs (135g), halved
- 1½ cups (375ml) fresh pure apple juice
- 2 medium oranges (480g), washed
- 1⅔ cups (265g) coconut sugar
- 5 eggs
- 2¾ cups (280g) almond meal
- 1 teaspoon gluten-free baking powder
- ¼ cup (20g) flaked almonds

TIPS

You can use mandarins instead of oranges. If you find the cakes are getting too brown, cover with foil during cooking. Serve cakes with Greek-style yoghurt, if you like.

1 Place figs and juice in a medium saucepan; stand for 2 hours. Remove figs with a slotted spoon; reserve juice in pan.

2 Fill another medium saucepan two-thirds with water, add whole oranges; bring to the boil. Reduce heat to a simmer. Cover oranges with the lid from a smaller saucepan to keep submerged; simmer for 2 hours, topping up with water if necessary to keep oranges submerged. Drain; cool to room temperature.

3 Preheat oven to 180°C/350°F. Line a 12-hole (⅓ cup/80ml) muffin pan with deep paper cases.

4 Cut oranges in half, discard any seeds. Process oranges (rind and flesh) until smooth. Add coconut sugar, eggs, almond meal and baking powder to the food processor, pulse until well combined. Spoon mixture into paper cases; place a fig, cut-side up, on top; sprinkle with almonds.

5 Bake cakes for 1 hour or until a skewer inserted in the centre comes out clean.

6 Meanwhile, simmer saucepan with apple juice over medium heat for 10 minutes or until syrupy.

7 Brush syrup over warm cakes. Serve immediately.

Plus
**DAIRY FREE
YEAST FREE**

Coffee choc & chia
MOUSSE

PREP + COOK TIME 30 MINUTES (+ REFRIGERATION) **SERVES** 4

You will need to start this recipe a day ahead.

- 400ml can coconut cream
- ½ cup (125ml) black coffee, at room temperature
- 1½ tablespoons white chia seeds
- ¼ cup (60ml) pure maple syrup
- 1 tablespoon cocoa powder, sifted
- 50g (1½-ounce) piece dark (semi-sweet) chocolate

TIPS

Make sure you don't shake the coconut cream can after chilling so you don't mix the cream on top back into the liquid. To make this recipe dairy-free, use dairy-free dark chocolate.

1 Refrigerate unopened can of coconut cream overnight.

2 Whisk coffee, chia seeds and half the maple syrup in a medium bowl. Cover; refrigerate overnight or until thick.

3 Open chilled can of coconut cream; spoon the thick cream on the surface into a small bowl of electric mixer. Refrigerate remaining cream for another use.

4 Beat coconut cream in a small bowl with an electric mixer until thick and creamy. Add cocoa and remaining maple syrup; beat until combined.

5 Layer chocolate cream coffee and chia mixture into four small serving glasses. Using a vegetable peeler, shave chocolate into curls. Serve mousse sprinkled with chocolate curls.

Cardamom & lemon cake
WITH VANILLA LABNE

PREP + COOK TIME 2 HOURS (+ REFRIGERATION & STANDING) **SERVES** 8

You will need to start the labne a day ahead.

- 9 egg whites
- 270g (8½ ounces) butter, melted
- 1½ cups (180g) almond meal
- 2¼ cups (360g) gluten-free icing (confectioners') sugar
- ¾ cup (100g) gluten-free plain (all-purpose) flour
- 1 tablespoon finely grated lemon rind
- 3 teaspoons ground cardamom

VANILLA LABNE

- 1 vanilla bean
- 1kg (2 pounds) Greek-style yoghurt
- ½ teaspoon salt
- 2 tablespoons caster (superfine) sugar

LEMON SYRUP

- ¾ cup (180ml) lemon juice
- 1½ cups (330g) caster (superfine) sugar
- 2 lemons (280g), zested

TIPS

Cake can be made 2 days ahead, store in an airtight container.

1 Make vanilla labne.

2 Preheat oven 160°C/325°F. Grease a deep 20cm (8-inch) round cake pan; line base and sides with baking paper.

3 Whisk egg whites, butter, almond meal, icing sugar, sifted flour, rind and cardamom in a large bowl until well combined. Pour mixture into pan.

4 Bake cake for 1 hour 40 minutes or until a skewer inserted comes out clean; cover with foil halfway through cooking to prevent overbrowning. Stand cake in pan for 10 minutes before turning top-side up on a wire rack over an oven tray.

5 Meanwhile, make lemon syrup. Pour hot lemon syrup over hot cake.

6 Serve cooled cake with vanilla labne and reserved syrup and zest.

vanilla labne Split vanilla bean in half lengthways; scrape seeds into a medium bowl. Discard pod. Add remaining ingredients; stir until combined. Spoon yoghurt mixture into a sieve lined with two layers of muslin (or a clean Chux cloth). Tie cloth close to yoghurt. Refrigerate 12 hours or overnight, squeezing the yoghurt occasionally, until thick. Stir yoghurt until smooth.

lemon syrup Stir ingredients in a small saucepan over medium heat until sugar dissolves. Bring to the boil; boil for 5 minutes or until syrup thickens. Remove from heat. Reserve 2 tablespoons syrup and zest.

**NUTRITIONAL
COUNT PER SERVING**
47.8g total fat
23.9g saturated fat
3708kJ (887 cal)
100.5g carbohydrate
15.7g protein
2.3g fibre

4 ways with
RAW BROWNIES

Plus
YEAST FREE
DAIRY FREE
EGG FREE

Plus
YEAST FREE
DAIRY FREE
EGG FREE

NUTRITIONAL COUNT PER BROWNIE
8.7g total fat
1.5g saturated fat
615kJ (147 cal)
14.7g carbohydrate
1.7g protein
3.1g fibre

NUTRITIONAL COUNT PER BROWNIE
10.7g total fat
1.2g saturated fat
726kJ (174 cal)
17.8g carbohydrate
2.4g protein
1.1g fibre

CITRUS & PISTACHIO RAW BROWNIES

PREP TIME 20 MINUTES (+ REFRIGERATION)

MAKES 27

Grease and line base and sides of a 20cm (8-inch) square cake pan with baking paper. Process 2¼ cups (270g) pecans until finely chopped. With motor operating, add 2¼ cups (520g) fresh pitted dates, ⅓ cup (35g) raw cacao powder, 3 teaspoons water, 1½ teaspoons coconut oil, 2 teaspoons finely grated orange rind and 2 teaspoons finely grated lemon rind; process until mixture comes together. Transfer to a bowl; stir in ½ cup (70g) chopped pistachios. Press mixture evenly into pan; press on ½ cup (70g) chopped pistachios. Refrigerate for 1 hour or until firm. Cut raw brownies into 27 fingers.

CRUNCHY WALNUT RAW BROWNIES

PREP TIME 20 MINUTES (+ REFRIGERATION)

MAKES 25

Grease and line base and sides of a 20cm (8-inch) square cake pan with baking paper. Process 2¼ cups (270g) pecans until finely chopped. With motor operating, add 2¼ cups (520g) fresh pitted dates, ⅓ cup (35g) raw cacao powder, 3 teaspoons water, 1½ teaspoons coconut oil and 1 teaspoon ground cinnamon; process until mixture comes together. Transfer to a bowl; stir in ½ cup (55g) chopped walnuts and ¼ cup (40g) cacao nibs. Press mixture evenly into pan; level with a palette knife. Refrigerate for 1 hour or until firm. Dust with 1 teaspoon cocoa powder. Cut raw brownies into 25 squares.

**NUTRITIONAL
COUNT PER BROWNIE**
16.2g total fat
2.1g saturated fat
1013kJ (242 cal)
18.8g carbohydrate
6.1g protein
1.1g fibre

Plus
**YEAST FREE
DAIRY FREE
EGG FREE**

Plus
**YEAST FREE
DAIRY FREE
EGG FREE**

**NUTRITIONAL
COUNT PER BROWNIE**
10.5g total fat
1.3g saturated fat
700kJ (167 cal)
14.5g carbohydrate
2.6g protein
3.5g fibre

DATE & RASPBERRY RAW BROWNIES

PREP TIME 20 MINUTES (+ REFRIGERATION)

MAKES 27

Grease and line base and sides of a 20cm (8-inch) square cake pan with baking paper. Process 2¼ cups (270g) pecans until finely chopped. With motor operating, add 2¼ cups (520g) fresh pitted dates, ⅓ cup raw cacao powder, 3 teaspoons water and 1½ teaspoons coconut oil; process until mixture comes together. Press mixture evenly into pan; level with a palette knife. Refrigerate for 1 hour or until firm. Drizzle with 50g (1½oz) melted 70% dark chocolate; top with 60g (2oz) raspberries. Cut raw brownies into 27 fingers.

PEANUT BUTTER & SEEDS RAW BROWNIES

PREP TIME 20 MINUTES (+ REFRIGERATION)

MAKES 25

Grease and line base and sides of a 20cm (8-inch) square cake pan with baking paper. Combine 2 tablespoons sesame seeds, 1 tablespoon linseeds and ⅓ cup (65g) pepitas (pumpkin seed kernels) in a small bowl. Process 2¼ cups (270g) pecans until finely chopped. With motor operating, add 2¼ cups (520g) fresh pitted dates, ⅓ cup (35g) raw cacao powder, 3 teaspoons water and 1½ teaspoons coconut oil; process until mixture comes together. Transfer to a bowl; stir in half the seed mixture. Press half the mixture into pan; top with ½ cup (140g) natural peanut butter, in teaspoonfuls. Press on remaining date mixture. Refrigerate for 1 hour or until firm. Spread top with an extra ½ cup (140g) natural peanut butter; sprinkle with remaining seed mixture. Refrigerate for 30 minutes or until firm. Cut raw brownies into 25 squares.

**NUTRITIONAL
COUNT PER CUPCAKE**
13.9g total fat
3.4g saturated fat
1250kJ (299 cal)
43.2g carbohydrate
1.9g protein
0.1g fibre

Vanilla CUPCAKES

PREP + COOK TIME 45 MINUTES (+ COOLING) **MAKES** 14

- 1 cup (220g) caster (superfine) sugar
- 1 teaspoon vanilla extract
- 3 eggs
- 125g (4 ounces) dairy-free spread
- 1½ cups (200g) gluten-free self-raising flour
- ½ cup (35g) gluten-free baby rice cereal
- ¼ cup (60ml) soy milk

VANILLA FROSTING

- 125g (4 ounces) dairy-free spread
- 1 teaspoon vanilla extract
- 1½ cups (240g) gluten-free icing (confectioners') sugar

1 Preheat oven to 180°C/350°F. Line 14 holes of two 12-hole (⅓-cup/80ml) muffin pans with paper cases.

2 Beat sugar, vanilla and eggs in a small bowl with an electric mixer for 5 minutes or until thick and pale. Add dairy-free spread, a little at a time, beating well between additions. Mixture may look curdled at this stage. Gradually add sifted flour, rice cereal and milk. Spoon mixture into paper cases.

3 Bake cupcakes for 20 minutes. Leave cupcakes in pan for 5 minutes before turning, top-side up, onto a wire rack to cool.

4 Meanwhile, make vanilla frosting.

5 Spread frosting over cooled cupcakes. Dust lightly with a little sifted cocoa, if you like.

vanilla frosting Beat dairy-free spread and vanilla in a small bowl with an electric mixer until pale. Beat in sifted icing sugar in two batches, until well combined and smooth.

VARIATIONS

blueberry cupcakes Stir in ¾ cup frozen blueberries to vanilla cupcake mixture after adding the soy milk.

coconut cherry cupcakes Stir in ¼ cup desiccated coconut, ½ cup sifted cocoa powder, ¼ cup soy milk, 100g (3 ounces) finely chopped red glacé cherries and ¼ cup (40g) finely chopped dairy-free dark chocolate into the vanilla cupcake mixture after adding the baby rice cereal. Make vanilla frosting recipe, with the following changes: After beating dairy-free spread and vanilla until pale, combine 1 cup sifted gluten-free icing (confectioners') sugar and ½ cup sifted cocoa powder; beat combined sifted mixture in two batches, until combined and smooth. Spread over cupcakes.

apple cinnamon cupcakes Stir in ⅓ cup coarsely chopped canned pie apple into the vanilla cupcake mixture after adding the soy milk. Combine 2 teaspoons ground cinnamon and 2 tablespoons gluten-free icing (confectioners') sugar; dust cupcakes with cinnamon mixture.

TIPS

Cupcakes are best served on the day of baking. Freeze uniced cakes in an airtight container for up to 3 months.

Honey yoghurt
ICE-CREAM LOAF

PREP + COOK TIME 40 MINUTES (+ FREEZING) SERVES 10

You will need to start this recipe a day ahead.

- 8 pitted medjool dates (120g), chopped coarsely
- 125g (4 ounces) pecans, chopped coarsely
- 2 tablespoons hulled tahini, at room temperature
- 1 tablespoon chopped glacé ginger
- 1 teaspoon ground cinnamon
- 1 tablespoon raw honey
- 2¾ cups (770g) Greek-style vanilla yoghurt
- 4 large ripe figs (320g), cut into wedges
- ⅓ cup (50g) shelled unsalted pistachios, chopped
- ¼ cup (90g) raw honey, extra

1 Grease and line a 10cm x 21cm (4-inch x 8½-inch) loaf pan with baking paper.

2 Blend or process dates and pecans until mixture resembles fine breadcrumbs. Add tahini, ginger and cinnamon; process until mixture just comes together. Press mixture firmly over base of pan.

3 Combine honey and yoghurt in a medium bowl. Spread yoghurt mixture over top of pecan mixture; freeze overnight or until firm.

4 Remove from freezer; stand at room temperature for 15 minutes. Turn out onto a serving plate; top with figs and pistachios; drizzle with extra honey.

TIPS

Walnuts or cashews can be substituted for pecans. Decorate with seasonal fruit if fresh figs aren't available.

**NUTRITIONAL
COUNT PER SERVING**
16.3g total fat
2.3g saturated fat
1313kJ (314 cal)
29.5g carbohydrate
9.7g protein
6.2g fibre

NUTRITIONAL
COUNT PER SERVING
31.2g total fat
27.5g saturated fat
1735kJ (415 cal)
27.4g carbohydrate
3.6g protein
7.4g fibre

Plus
NUT FREE
DAIRY FREE
YEAST FREE
EGG FREE

Coconut bark with
FRAGRANT FRUIT SALAD

PREP + COOK TIME 30 MINUTES (+ COOLING & FREEZING) **SERVES** 4

- 400ml can coconut cream
- 2 tablespoons coconut oil
- ½ teaspoon vanilla extract
- 1 tablespoon desiccated coconut, toasted
- 200g (6½ ounces) blueberries
- 200g (6½ ounces) raspberries
- 2 medium peaches (300g), seeded, sliced
- ½ small ripe red papaya (200g), peeled, cut into wedges
- 1 tablespoon fresh small mint leaves

SYRUP

- 2 tablespoons caster (superfine) sugar
- ⅓ cup (80ml) water
- ½ teaspoon rosewater
- 1 teaspoon vanilla extract

1 Make syrup.

2 Meanwhile, line a baking tray with baking paper. Scoop the coconut cream from the top of the can into a small bowl; you will need 1 cup (250ml). Add coconut oil and vanilla; whisk until well combined.

3 Spread the coconut mixture on tray; sprinkle with desiccated coconut. Freeze for 30 minutes or until firm. Cut or break bark into large shards.

4 Place fruit in bowls; drizzle with syrup and top with mint. Serve fruit salad with coconut bark.

syrup Stir sugar and the water in a small saucepan over medium heat until sugar is dissolved. Bring to the boil; simmer for 5 minutes. Remove from heat; stir in rosewater and vanilla. Cool.

Baby lemon MERINGUE TARTS

PREP + COOK TIME 1 HOUR (+ REFRIGERATION) MAKES 12

- 1 cup (100g) almond meal
- 2 tablespoons brown rice flour
- 1½ tablespoons pure maple syrup
- ½ teaspoon vanilla extract
- 1½ tablespoons coconut oil
- 2 teaspoons apple cider vinegar
- 2 teaspoons water
- 2 egg whites
- ½ cup (110g) caster (superfine) sugar

LEMON CURD

- 1 egg
- 1 egg yolk
- 2 teaspoons finely grated lemon rind
- ¼ cup (60ml) lemon juice
- 1 tablespoon pure maple syrup
- 1 teaspoon vanilla extract
- 60g (2 ounces) butter, chopped

1 Make lemon curd.

2 Preheat oven to 160°C/325°F. Grease a 12-hole (1½ tablespoon/30ml) shallow round-based patty pan.

3 Process or blend almond meal, brown rice flour, maple syrup and vanilla until combined. Add coconut oil, vinegar and the water; process until mixture forms a ball. Divide pastry into 12 equal portions. Press pastry evenly into holes of pan.

4 Bake for 20 minutes or until crisp and golden. Cool.

5 Increase oven to 190°C/375°F.

6 Divide curd among tart shells.

7 Beat egg whites in a medium bowl with an electric mixer until soft peaks form. Gradually add sugar, beating until dissolved. Spoon meringue over curd. Return to oven for 2 minutes or until meringue is lightly browned.

lemon curd Place ingredients in a medium heatproof bowl; stir over a saucepan of simmering water (ensuring base of bowl does not touch the water) for 10 minutes or until mixture thickly coats the back of a wooden spoon. Cover surface with plastic wrap; cool. Refrigerate for 2 hours or until cold.

TIPS

If you have a kitchen blowtorch,
you can use it to brown the meringues.

**NUTRITIONAL
COUNT PER TART**
11.9g total fat
5.3g saturated fat
751kJ (179 cal)
15.1g carbohydrate
3.4g protein
0.8g fibre

**NUTRITIONAL
COUNT PER SERVING**
10.4g total fat
7.8g saturated fat
1427kJ (341 cal)
58.4g carbohydrate
3.3g protein
2.5g fibre

Banana & warm spice
RASPBERRY BREAD

PREP + COOK TIME 1¼ HOURS **SERVES** 8

*You will need 2 large (460g) overripe bananas
for this recipe.*

- 1½ cups (200g) gluten-free plain (all-purpose) flour
- 1 teaspoon gluten-free baking powder
- 1 teaspoon bicarbonate soda (baking soda)
- 1 teaspoon ground cinnamon
- 1 teaspoon ground cardamom
- ½ teaspoon ground ginger
- ¼ teaspoon ground nutmeg
- 1 cup (75g) shredded coconut
- 1 cup (220g) firmly packed brown sugar
- 1 tablespoon coconut oil
- 1 egg
- ⅓ cup (80ml) almond milk
- 1 cup (280g) ripe mashed bananas
- 125g (4½ ounces) raspberries

1 Preheat oven to 170°C/335°F. Grease and line a 13cm x 23cm (5¼-inch x 9¼-inch) loaf pan with baking paper.
2 Sift flour, baking powder, bicarbonate soda and spices into a large bowl; stir in coconut and sugar. Make a well in the centre. Whisk coconut oil, egg and milk in a medium bowl. Add egg mixture to flour mixture; mix to combine. Fold in banana and three-quarters of the raspberries. Pour into pan; top with remaining raspberries.
3 Bake bread for 45 minutes or until a skewer comes out clean when inserted into centre. Leave in pan for 15 minutes; turn out onto a wire rack to cool completely. Serve.

This bread is best made on the day of serving. Leftovers can be grilled (broiled) until toasted. Bread will freeze up to 3 months.

Peanut butter COOKIES

PREP + COOK TIME 20 MINUTES (+ COOLING) **MAKES** 21

- 1 cup (280g) crunchy natural peanut butter
- ⅔ cup (150g) firmly packed brown sugar
- 1 egg, beaten lightly
- 1 teaspoon gluten-free baking powder
- 1 teaspoon vanilla extract
- ½ teaspoon sea salt flakes

1 Preheat oven to 180°C/350°F. Line two baking trays with baking paper.

2 Using a fork, mix peanut butter, sugar, egg, baking powder and vanilla in a medium bowl until well combined.

3 Shape level tablespoons of mixture into balls; place on trays 3cm (1¼ inches) apart. Flatten slightly with a fork; sprinkle with lightly crumbled salt.

4 Bake cookies for 10 minutes or until crisp and golden. Cool on trays.

TIPS

Cookies will keep in an airtight container for up to 1 week.

**NUTRITIONAL
COUNT PER COOKIE**
7.2g total fat
1.3g saturated fat
468kJ (112 cal)
8.3g carbohydrate
3.6g protein
0.9g fibre

**NUTRITIONAL
COUNT PER SERVING**
18g total fat
9.8g saturated fat
1233kJ (295 cal)
26.8g carbohydrate
5.7g protein
2.1g fibre

Rustic FRUIT PIE

PREP + COOK TIME 50 MINUTES (+ REFRIGERATION) **SERVES** 8

- ⅔ cup (90g) gluten-free plain (all-purpose) flour
- ½ cup (80g) coconut flour
- ⅓ cup (40g) almond meal
- 2 tablespoons gluten-free icing (confectioners') sugar
- 125g (4 ounces) chilled butter, chopped
- 1 egg
- 1 tablespoon ice cold water, approximately (see tips)
- 750g (1½ pounds) peaches, peeled, sliced
- 250g (8 ounces) strawberries
- 1 tablespoon vanilla sugar
- 3 teaspoons finely grated lemon rind
- 1 egg yolk

TIPS

Peaches can be swapped with plums
or nectarines. When making pastry,
add a little water at a time; depending
on the batch of gluten-free flour,
you may need less or more water.

1 Preheat oven to 180°C/350°F. Grease a 23cm (9-inch) pie dish.

2 Blend or process flours, almond meal and icing sugar until just combined. Add butter, process until mixture resembles breadcrumbs. Add egg, process until combined. Add enough water to form a ball.

3 Tip mixture onto a sheet of plastic wrap, bring together into a disc. Wrap mixture; refrigerate for 15 minutes.

4 Combine peaches and strawberries with sugar and rind in a medium bowl; toss to coat. Spoon fruit mixture into dish.

5 Roll pastry between two sheets of baking paper to form a circle big enough to cover top of dish. Carefully peel top sheet of baking paper from pastry, and using the bottom sheet, invert pastry disc on top of pie. Carefully remove baking paper; trim edges. Brush with egg yolk.

6 Bake pie for 30 minutes or until pastry is crisp and golden. Stand for 10 minutes before serving. Serve with gluten-free ice-cream or custard, if you like.

Teff fruit & NUT MUFFINS

PREP + COOK TIME 1 HOUR **MAKES** 12

- 1 cup (100g) walnuts halves
- ½ cup (125ml) macadamia oil
- 3 eggs
- 1 teaspoon mixed spice
- 1 teaspoon gluten-free baking powder
- ½ cup (65g) ivory or brown teff flour
- ½ cup (110g) raw caster (superfine) sugar
- ½ cup (60g) almond meal
- ½ cup (75g) dried apricots, chopped coarsely
- 1 cup (140g) chopped pitted medjool dates
- 1 small orange sweet potato (140g), grated coarsely
- ⅓ cup (25g) shredded coconut
- 2 tablespoons honey

1 Preheat oven to 180°C/350°F. Line a 12-hole (⅓-cup/80ml) muffin pan with paper cases.
2 Reserve 12 walnuts; coarsely chop remaining walnuts. Combine oil and eggs in a large jug.
3 Sift spice, baking powder and flour into a large bowl. Stir in sugar, almond meal, apricot, dates, sweet potato, coconut and chopped walnuts until well combined. Make a well in the centre, add oil mixture; stir until just combined. Spoon mixture into paper cases; top with reserved walnuts.
4 Bake muffins for 30 minutes or until a skewer comes out clean when inserted into the centre. Transfer to a wire rack to cool. Drizzle muffins with honey.

TIPS

Teff flour is available from health food stores. Muffins are best eaten warm. You can reheat them in the microwave on HIGH (100%) in 5 second bursts until warm.

NUTRITIONAL COUNT PER MUFFIN
21.1g total fat
3.5g saturated fat
1379kJ (330 cal)
29.3g carbohydrate
5.5g protein
3.6g fibre

Plus
**DAIRY FREE
YEAST FREE**

Plus

NUT FREE
DAIRY FREE
YEAST FREE
EGG FREE

NUTRITIONAL COUNT PER POPSICLE
11.4g total fat
6.3g saturated fat
662kJ (158 cal)
12.8g carbohydrate
1.4g protein
1.5g fibre

Avocado chocolate
POPSICLES

PREP + COOK TIME 20 MINUTES (+ FREEZING) **MAKES** 6

- 2 tablespoons cacao powder
- 2 tablespoons coconut cream
- ⅓ cup (80ml) pure maple syrup
- 1 small avocado (200g), peeled, stone discarded
- ½ cup (125ml) coconut cream, extra

1 Combine cacao, coconut cream and 2 tablespoons of maple syrup into a small bowl. Spoon mixture into six ⅓-cup (80ml) capacity popsicle moulds.

2 Blend or process avocado, extra coconut cream and remaining maple syrup until smooth. Spoon mixture into popsicle moulds. Use a popsicle stick to push mixture down into the moulds and to remove any air pockets. Push popsicle sticks into each mould. Freeze for at least 4 hours or overnight.

3 Dip popsicle moulds briefly in boiling water; remove popsicles. Serve sprinkled with toasted shredded coconut, if you like.

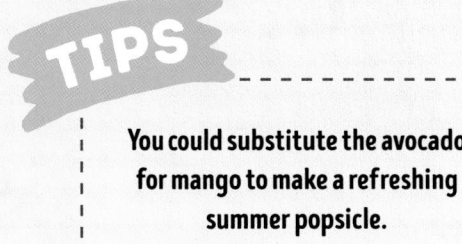

TIPS

You could substitute the avocado for mango to make a refreshing summer popsicle.

Raw lime & white
CHOCOLATE CASHEW TARTS

PREP TIME 40 MINUTES (+ STANDING & REFRIGERATION) MAKES 12

You will need to start this recipe a day ahead.

- 1 cup (140g) macadamias
- ¼ cup (30g) almond meal
- 2 tablespoons macadamia oil
- 1 teaspoon vanilla extract
- 20g (¾ ounce) white chocolate, grated coarsely
- 1 medium lime (90g)

LIME FILLING

- 1½ cups (225g) raw cashews
- ½ cup (45g) desiccated coconut
- ¼ cup (60ml) coconut cream
- 2 teaspoons finely grated lime rind
- 2 tablespoons lime juice
- 2 tablespoons pure maple syrup
- 50g (1½ ounces) white chocolate, chopped

1 Grease a 12-hole (⅓-cup/80ml) muffin pan. Line holes with a strip of baking paper that lines base and sides and extends 2cm (¾ inch) above the edge.

2 Blend or process macadamias, almond meal, oil and vanilla until mixture comes together. Divide mixture into 12 portions. Press each portion into the base of pan holes, pressing firmly. Refrigerate until needed.

3 Meanwhile, make lime filling. Spoon filling over bases; refrigerate for 3 hours or until set.

4 Top tarts with grated chocolate. Using a zester, remove rind from lime; sprinkle over tarts. Stand at room temperature for 15 minutes before serving.

lime filling Place cashews in a medium bowl; cover with cold water. Stand overnight; drain. Blend or process cashews with coconut, coconut cream, rind, juice and maple syrup until smooth. Stir in white chocolate.

TIPS

You will need to carefully run a knife around the edge to loosen the tarts or wipe the base of the pan with a hot cloth to turn them out. You can also use a silicone muffin pan if you prefer.

Plus

YEAST FREE EGG FREE

**NUTRITIONAL
COUNT PER TART**
33g total fat
8.8g saturated fat
1553kJ (372 cal)
12.3g carbohydrate
6.1g protein
2.3g fibre

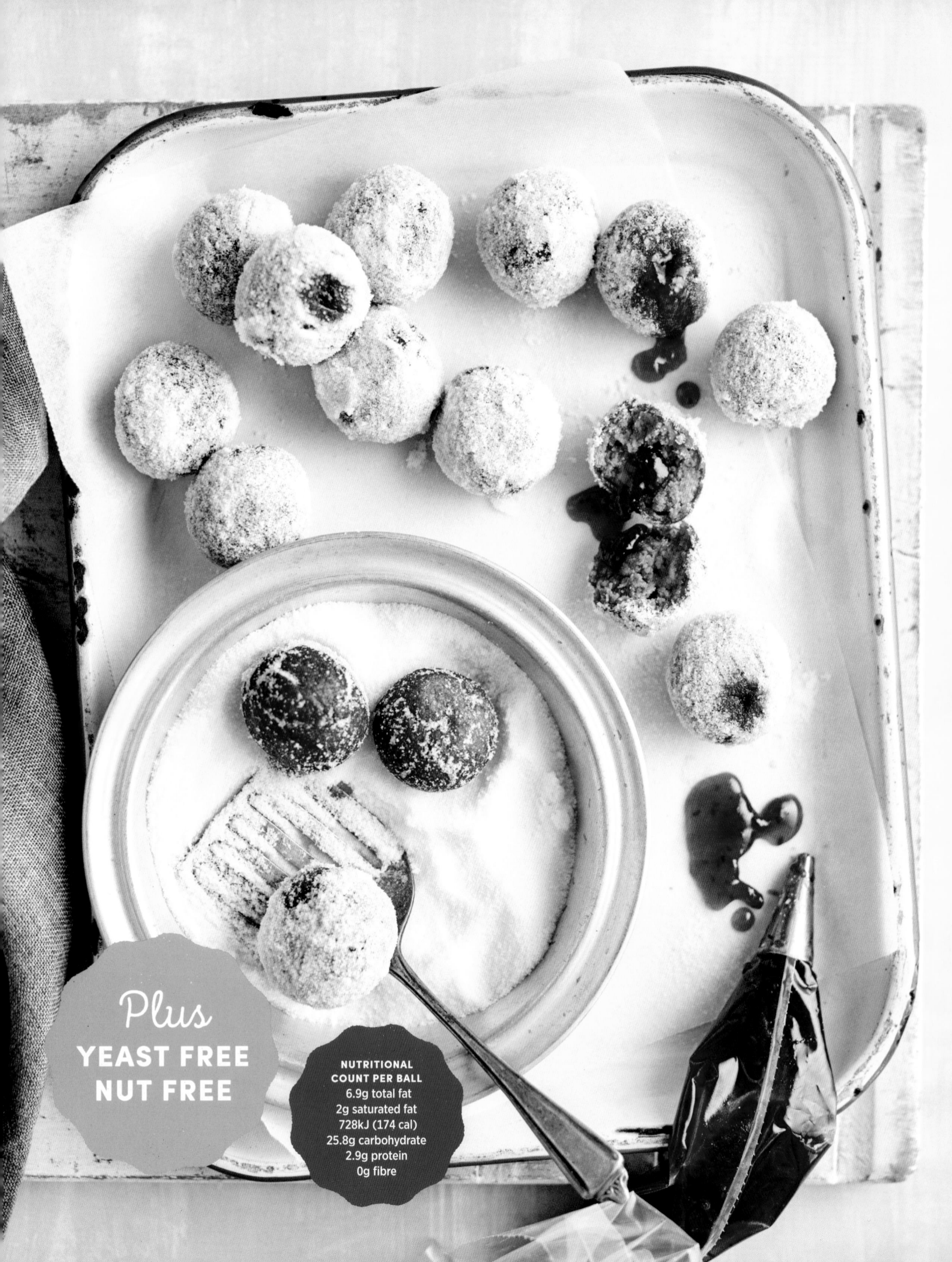

**NUTRITIONAL
COUNT PER BALL**
6.9g total fat
2g saturated fat
728kJ (174 cal)
25.8g carbohydrate
2.9g protein
0g fibre

Raspberry-filled
RICOTTA BALLS

PREP + COOK TIME 20 MINUTES MAKES 10

- 1 egg
- ⅓ cup (55g) coconut sugar
- ½ teaspoon bicarbonate soda (baking soda)
- 125g (4 ounces) smooth ricotta
- ¼ cup (35g) gluten-free plain (all-purpose) flour
- ¼ cup (40g) coconut flour
- vegetable oil, for deep-frying
- 2 tablespoons raspberry jam
- ½ cup (110g) caster (superfine) sugar

1 Beat egg and coconut sugar in a small bowl with an electric mixer until combined. Add soda, ricotta and flours; beat until smooth. Shape rounded teaspoons of mixture into balls.

2 Heat vegetable oil in a large heavy-based saucepan over medium-high heat until oil reaches 160°C/320°F on a sugar (candy) thermometer (or until a drop of mixture floats to the surface). Deep-fry balls, in batches, for 2½ minutes or until browned lightly and cooked through. Drain on paper towel. Stand until cool enough to handle.

3 Make a small hole in top of each ball, using a small sharp knife. Spoon or pipe jam into balls; roll in sugar. Serve warm.

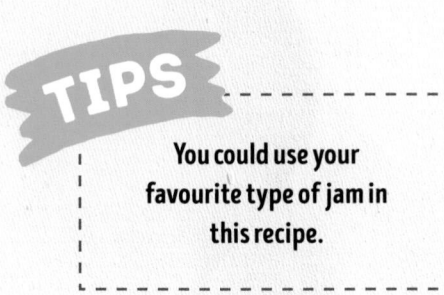

TIPS

You could use your favourite type of jam in this recipe.

Salted chocolate cake
WITH PEANUT MAPLE ICING

PREP + COOK TIME 1 HOUR (+ COOLING) **SERVES** 10

- ½ cup (50g) cocoa powder
- ½ cup (125ml) boiling water
- 1 teaspoon sea salt flakes
- 2 teaspoons vanilla extract
- 1 cup (160g) coconut sugar
- 3 eggs
- ⅔ cup (160ml) olive oil
- 1½ cups (180g) almond meal
- ⅓ cup (80ml) pure maple syrup
- ½ cup (140g) smooth natural peanut butter
- 1 tablespoon pure maple syrup, extra
- sea salt flakes, extra

1 Preheat oven to 180°C/350°F. Grease and line base of a 20cm (8-inch) springform pan with baking paper.

2 Whisk sifted cocoa, the water, salt and vanilla in a jug until combined.

3 Beat coconut sugar, eggs and oil in a small bowl with an electric mixer until creamy. Add almond meal and cocoa mixture; stir until smooth. Pour into pan.

4 Bake cake for 45 minutes or until a skewer comes out almost clean when inserted into centre. Cool cake in pan.

5 Combine maple syrup and peanut butter in a small bowl. Spread over top of cake. Serve cake drizzled with extra maple syrup; sprinkled with extra salt.

TIPS

Swap smooth peanut butter for crunchy, if you like. Uniced cake can be frozen for up to 3 months.

Basic COOKIES

PREP + COOK TIME 25 MINUTES (+ REFRIGERATION & COOLING) **MAKES** 24

- 250g (8 ounces) butter, softened
- 1 cup (220g) firmly packed brown sugar
- 2 teaspoon vanilla extract
- 2 eggs
- 2½ cups (340g) gluten-free plain (all-purpose) flour
- ⅓ cup (60g) white rice flour
- 1 teaspoon bicarbonate of soda (baking soda)
- 2 teaspoons xanthan gum

1 Preheat oven to 180°C/350°F. Line four oven trays with baking paper.

2 Beat butter, sugar and vanilla in a medium bowl with an electric mixer until just combined. Add eggs; beat until just combined. Stir in sifted flours, soda and gum, in two batches. Cover; refrigerate for 1 hour.

3 Using wet hands, roll dough into 24 balls. Flatten balls to 6cm (2½ inches); place 5cm (2 inches) apart on trays.

4 Bake cookies for 18 minutes or until golden. Cool on trays.

TIPS

Cookies can be stored in an airtight container for up to 1 week.

4 ways with
ICE-CREAM SANDWICHES

Plus
**YEAST FREE
NUT FREE**

Plus
**YEAST FREE
NUT FREE**

**NUTRITIONAL
COUNT PER
SANDWICH**
19.1g total fat
12.2g saturated fat
1660kJ (397 cal)
53g carbohydrate
3.8g protein
0.6g fibre

**NUTRITIONAL
COUNT PER
SANDWICH**
21.3g total fat
14.1g saturated fat
1737kJ (416 cal)
52.9g carbohydrate
3.9g protein
0.2g fibre

VERY BERRY
ICE-CREAM SANDWICHES

PREP + COOK TIME 45 MINUTES

(+ REFRIGERATION & FREEZING) MAKES 6

Make basic cookies from page 215. Place ½ cup (70g) mixed frozen berries in a medium bowl. Stand for 10 minutes or until slightly thawed; crush lightly. Stir in 1½ cups 97% fat-free no-added sugar vanilla ice-cream. Transfer ice-cream mixture to a freezer-proof container. Freeze for 1 hour or until firm. Sandwich scoops of ice-cream between cookies.

TIP Allow the ice-cream to soften slightly before stirring in the ingredients.

COCONUT & LIME
ICE-CREAM SANDWICHES

PREP + COOK TIME 40 MINUTES

(+ REFRIGERATION & FREEZING) MAKES 6

Make basic cookies from page 215. Combine 1 tablespoon toasted shredded coconut, 2 teaspoons finely grated lime rind and 1½ cups 97% fat-free no-added sugar vanilla ice-cream in a medium bowl. Transfer ice-cream to a freezer-proof container. Freeze for 1 hour or until firm. Sandwich scoops of ice-cream between cookies.

TIP Allow the ice-cream to soften slightly before stirring in the ingredients.

Plus
YEAST FREE

NUTRITIONAL COUNT PER SANDWICH
21.5g total fat
12.3g saturated fat
1741kJ (417 cal);
52.4g carbohydrate
4.2g protein
0.6g fibre

Plus
YEAST FREE
NUT FREE

NUTRITIONAL COUNT PER SANDWICH
19.2g total fat
12.2g saturated fat
1796kJ (430 cal)
61.5g carbohydrate
3.9g protein
0.2g fibre

COFFEE & HAZELNUT ICE-CREAM SANDWICHES

PREP + COOK TIME 45 MINUTES
(+ REFRIGERATION & FREEZING) MAKES 6

Make basic cookies from page 215. Combine 1 tablespoon cold espresso coffee, 2 tablespoons finely chopped toasted hazelnuts and 1½ cups 97% fat-free no-added sugar vanilla ice-cream in a medium bowl. Transfer ice-cream to a freezer-proof container. Freeze for 1 hour or until firm. Sandwich scoops of ice-cream between cookies.

TIP Allow the ice-cream to soften slightly before stirring in the ingredients.

CARAMEL SWIRL ICE-CREAM SANDWICHES

PREP + COOK TIME 40 MINUTES
(+ REFRIGERATION & FREEZING) MAKES 6

Make basic cookies from page 215. Place 1½ cups 97% fat-free no-added sugar vanilla ice-cream in a freezer-proof container. Swirl in ¼ cup gluten-free caramel sauce. Freeze for 1 hour or until firm. Sandwich scoops of ice-cream between cookies.

TIP Allow the ice-cream to soften slightly before stirring in the ingredients.

Sesame seed chocolate
BUBBLE SLICE

PREP + COOK TIME 20 MINUTES (+ REFRIGERATION) **MAKES** 18

You will need to start this recipe a day ahead.

- 2 tablespoons coconut oil
- 10 pitted medjool dates (200g), chopped coarsely
- ½ cup (140g) natural crunchy peanut butter
- ⅓ cup (90g) hulled tahini, at room temperature
- 1 teaspoon ground cinnamon
- ¼ cup (50g) pepitas (pumpkin seed kernels)
- ¼ cup (35g) sunflower seeds
- 2 tablespoons black sesame seeds
- ¼ cup (30g) goji berries
- ⅔ cup (18g) puffed quinoa
- 200g (6½ ounces) dark chocolate (semi-sweet), melted
- 1 tablespoon coconut oil, extra, melted

1 Grease an 18cm x 27.5cm (7¼-inch x 11-inch) slice pan; line base and sides with baking paper.

2 Cook coconut oil, dates, peanut butter and tahini in a medium saucepan, over medium heat, for 5 minutes until melted and combined. Transfer to a large heatproof bowl; stir in cinnamon, seeds, goji berries and quinoa. Press mixture into pan.

3 Pour combined chocolate and extra coconut oil over slice; refrigerate overnight or until firm. Cut into 18 pieces.

TIPS

Store slice in an airtight container in the fridge. Puffed quinoa is available from health food stores, you can substitute with puffed rice, if you like. Use only the thick, non-oily part of the tahini and peanut butter to keep the base firm.

NUTRITIONAL
COUNT PER SERVING
18.3g total fat
6.5g saturated fat
1090kJ (260 cal)
17.3g carbohydrate
6g protein
3.7g fibre

Plus
YEAST FREE
EGG FREE

Berry-licious
BLISS BALLS

PREP + COOK TIME 20 MINUTES MAKES 24

- 1 cup (250g) pitted medjool dates, chopped
- 1 cup (160g) natural almonds
- 1 cup (130g) dried cranberries
- 2 tablespoons cacao powder
- ½ cup (60g) goji berries
- 2 tablespoons shredded coconut

1 Blend or process dates, almonds, cranberries, cacao and goji berries until mixture comes together.

2 Shape tablespoons of the mixture into balls; wet your hands every third or fourth ball to stop the mixture from sticking. Coat the balls in coconut.

TIPS

These bliss balls will keep in an airtight container for up to 3 days.

Pumpkin PIE

PREP + COOK TIME 2 HOURS 10 MINUTES (+ REFRIGERATION & COOLING) **SERVES** 10

You will need to start this recipe a day ahead.

- 400ml can coconut cream
- 1.5kg (3-pound) jap pumpkin, cut into thick wedges
- 4 eggs
- ½ cup (125ml) pure maple syrup
- ½ cup (125ml) thickened (heavy) cream
- 1 teaspoon vanilla extract
- 1 teaspoon ground cinnamon
- ½ teaspoon ground nutmeg
- ½ teaspoon ground allspice
- ½ teaspoon ground ginger
- 2 teaspoons gluten-free icing (confectioners') sugar
- ¼ cup (35g) roasted hazelnuts, chopped coarsely

PASTRY

- ¼ cup (40g) brown rice flour
- 1½ cups (150g) hazelnut meal
- 2 tablespoons black or white chia seeds
- 2 medjool dates (40g), pitted
- 2½ tablespoons pure maple syrup
- 40g (1½ ounces) butter, melted
- 1 tablespoon water

TIPS

Leftover roast pumpkin can be used
in salads, pastas or risottos.

1 Refrigerate unopened can of coconut cream overnight.

2 Preheat oven to 160°C/325°F. Lightly grease a 24cm (9½-inch) pie dish.

3 Make pastry.

4 Increase oven temperature to 180°C/350°F.

5 Place pumpkin on a baking-paper-lined oven tray. Bake for 45 minutes or until pumpkin is tender. Cool.

6 Blend or process 3 cups of cooled pumpkin flesh until smooth. Add eggs, one at a time, processing after each addition. Add maple syrup, cream, vanilla and spices; process until well combined. Pour pumpkin mixture into pastry case.

7 Bake pie for 45 minutes or until set. Cool.

8 Without shaking the can, open chilled can of coconut cream; spoon the thick cream on the surface into a small bowl (store remaining coconut cream for another use). Beat with an electric mixer until thick and creamy.

9 Dust pie with sifted icing sugar. Serve with whipped coconut cream and hazelnuts.

pastry Process all ingredients until mixture forms a ball. Roll out pastry between two sheets of baking paper until 5mm (¼-inch) thick. Peel off top sheet of paper and invert pastry into tin. Carefully remove remaining baking paper; press pastry into base and sides of tin, trim edges. Line pastry with baking paper; fill with dried beans or rice. Bake for 20 minutes or until dry around the edge. Remove paper and beans; bake a further 5 minutes or until pastry case is completely dry, covering edges with foil if over browning.

NUTRITIONAL
COUNT PER SERVING
25.4g total fat
8.6g saturated fat
1547kJ (370 cal)
26.8g carbohydrate
7.7g protein
4.9g fibre

Chocolate & almond
COOKIES

PREP + COOK TIME 30 MINUTES **MAKES** 24

- ⅓ cup (80ml) almond oil
- ⅔ cup (190g) almond spread
- ⅔ cup (150g) firmly packed brown sugar
- ⅓ cup (35g) cocoa powder
- ¼ cup (35g) slivered almonds, chopped
- 1½ cups (200g) gluten-free plain (all-purpose) flour

1 Preheat oven to 160°C/325°F. Grease two baking trays and line with baking paper.

2 In a large bowl, mix oil, spread and sugar using a fork until combined. Add remaining ingredients; stir until mixture forms a soft dough.

3 Roll tablespoons of mixture into balls. Place on baking trays, 3cm (1¼ inches) apart. Press to flatten slightly with a lightly greased fork.

4 Bake for 20 minutes or until firm. Cool cookies on trays for 10 minutes. Transfer to a wire rack; cool completely.

TIPS

You can substitute the almond oil and nuts with any other nut or nut oil. For choc-chip cookies, add 100g (3 ounces) chopped dark chocolate to the mixture. Store biscuits in an airtight container for up to 1 week.

Rosemary, pear & BLUEBERRY CAKE

PREP + COOK TIME 1 HOUR 20 MINUTES (+ COOLING) **SERVES** 10

- 2 cups (270g) gluten-free plain (all-purpose) flour
- 1 teaspoon gluten-free baking powder
- ½ cup (60g) almond meal
- 250g (8 ounces) butter, softened
- 1 cup (160g) coconut sugar
- 1 teaspoon chopped fresh rosemary leaves
- 1 teaspoon vanilla extract
- 2 tablespoons pure maple syrup
- 4 eggs
- 1 cup (280g) Greek-style yoghurt
- 2 small ripe pears (360g), peeled, cored, sliced thinly
- 100g (3 ounces) blueberries
- ⅓ cup (80ml) pure maple syrup, extra

1 Preheat oven to 180°C/350°F. Grease and line a 24cm (9½-inch) springform pan.

2 Sift flour and baking powder into a medium bowl; stir in almond meal.

3 Beat butter and coconut sugar in a small bowl with an electric mixer until light and fluffy. Add rosemary, vanilla and maple syrup; beat until combined. Add eggs, one at a time, beating well after each addition. Fold in flour mixture and yoghurt. Spread mixture into pan; press sliced pear and blueberries on top.

4 Bake cake for 1 hour or until a skewer inserted into centre comes out clean. Cool in pan. Serve cake drizzled with extra maple syrup.

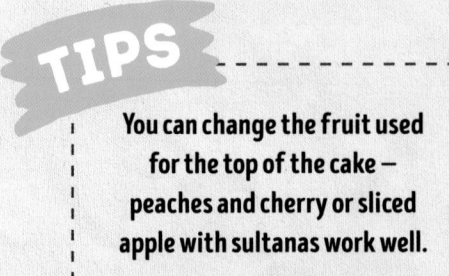

TIPS

You can change the fruit used for the top of the cake — peaches and cherry or sliced apple with sultanas work well.

**NUTRITIONAL
COUNT PER SERVING**
27.9g total fat
15.5g saturated fat
2102kJ (502 cal)
56.8g carbohydrate
6.4g protein
2.7g fibre

Christmas puddings
WITH BRANDY & GINGER

PREP + COOK TIME 6 HOURS (+ REFRIGERATION) **MAKES** 2 (SERVES 16)

You will need to start this recipe a day ahead.

- 350g (11 ounces) dried raisins
- 150g (4½ ounces) dried apricots, chopped
- 350g (11 ounces) sultanas
- 150g (4½ ounces) dried figs, chopped
- 100g (3 ounces) glacé ginger, chopped
- ⅔ cup (160ml) brandy
- 6 eggs
- 1 cup (160g) coconut sugar
- 2 medium apples (300g), grated coarsely
- 1½ tablespoons finely grated orange rind
- ¼ cup (60ml) orange juice
- 250g (8 ounces) ghee or butter, melted
- 1½ cups (195g) gluten-free breadcrumbs
- 2 teaspoons mixed spice

TIPS

If you only wish to make one pudding, halve the recipe. Puddings can be cooked ahead of time and reheated in steamers for 1 hour on the day of serving. Store puddings wrapped in plastic in the refrigerator, for up to 3 months or freeze.

1 Combine dried fruit and brandy into a large bowl. Cover; refrigerate overnight or longer if time permits.

2 Grease two 1.5 litre (6-cup) pudding basins or steamers. Line bases with a small round of baking paper. Place 30cm x 40cm (12-inch x 16-inch) piece of baking paper on top of a piece of foil cut the same size; fold a 5cm (2-inch) pleat crossways through the centre. Repeat to make two.

3 Beat eggs and sugar in a small bowl with electric mixer until thick and pale. Stir in fruit mixture with apple, rind, juice, ghee, breadcrumbs and spice until combined.

4 Spoon mixture evenly into basins, top puddings with the pleated baking paper and foil (this allows puddings to expand as they cook); secure with kitchen string (or lid).

5 Place an inverted saucer in the base of two large saucepans; place pudding basins on each saucer. Pour enough boiling water into pans to come halfway up the side of the basins; cover with tight-fitting lids. Boil puddings for 5 hours, replenishing with boiling water as necessary to maintain water level.

6 Remove puddings from water. Stand for 5 minutes before turning out. Serve puddings topped with gluten-free custard and fresh raspberries; dust with gluten-free icing (confectioners') sugar, if you like.

Banana & BEETROOT SORBET

PREP + COOK TIME 15 MINUTES (+ FREEZING) SERVES 4

- 4 medium frozen bananas (800g), broken into pieces
- 500g (1 pound) frozen strawberries
- 1 small beetroot (beets) (100g), peeled, chopped
- 1 tablespoon finely grated fresh ginger
- 2 cups (500ml) unsweetened almond milk
- 1 tablespoon white chia seeds
- 250g (8 ounces) fresh strawberries
- 2 medium golden kiwifruits (170g), cut into pieces

1 Working in two batches, place frozen bananas and strawberries, with beetroot, ginger and almond milk in a blender; blend until smooth.

2 Pour mixture into a freezer-proof container; cover with plastic wrap. Freeze for 6 hours or overnight until firm.

3 Working in two batches, scoop sorbet into blender; blend until smooth.

4 Pour sorbet into serving bowls or jars; top with chia seeds. Thread fresh strawberries and kiwifruit pieces onto wooden skewers. Serve sorbet immediately with fresh fruit skewers.

TIPS

Keep chopped bananas in a resealable plastic bag in the freezer to make early morning blending faster and easier. You can replace almond milk with any milk you prefer. Serve the sorbet with any of your favourite seasonal fruit. Sorbet can be stored in the freezer for up to 1 week.

**NUTRITIONAL
COUNT PER SERVING**
15.8g total fat
1g saturated fat
1466kJ (350 cal)
36.4g carbohydrate
10.8g protein
10.5g fibre

Plus
**DAIRY FREE
YEAST FREE
EGG FREE**

GLOSSARY

acai powder pronounced ah-sigh-EE; a small, round fruit with a large, hard, inedible pit and a dark purple, pulpy skin, that tastes like a blend of berries and chocolate. It supposedly has a high concentration of antioxidants, although further scientific studies are needed.

agave syrup a sweetener commercially produced from the agave plant in South Africa and Mexico. It is sweeter than sugar, though less viscous, so it dissolves quickly.

allspice so-named because it tastes like a combination of cumin, nutmeg, clove and cinnamon.

almonds

flaked paper-thin slices.

meal also called ground almonds.

slivered small pieces cut lengthways.

baking paper also called baking parchment or parchment paper; a silicone-coated paper primarily used to line baking pans and oven trays so cooked food doesn't stick.

baking powder, gluten-free a raising agent; readily available from supermarkets.

beans

black also called turtle beans or black kidney beans; an earthy-flavoured dried bean completely different from the better-known Chinese black beans (fermented soybeans). Used mostly in Mexican and South American cooking.

broad (fava) available dried, fresh, canned and frozen. Fresh should be peeled twice (discarding both the outer long green pod and the beige-green tough inner shell); the frozen beans have had their pods removed but the beige shell still needs removal.

green also known as french or string beans (although the tough string they once had has generally been bred out of them), this long thin fresh bean is consumed in its entirety once cooked.

kidney medium-size red bean, slightly floury in texture yet sweet in flavour; sold dried or canned, it's found in bean mixes and is used in chilli con carne.

sprouts tender new growths of assorted beans and seeds germinated for consumption as sprouts. Use in salads or as a filling for sandwiches.

beetroot (beets) firm, round root vegetable.

bicarbonate of soda (baking soda) used as a leavening agent in baking.

broccolini a cross between broccoli and chinese kale; it has long asparagus-like stems with a long loose floret, both are edible. Resembles broccoli but is milder and sweeter in taste.

buckwheat a herb in the same plant family as rhubarb; not a cereal so it is gluten-free. Available as flour; ground (cracked) into coarse, medium or fine granules (kasha) and used similarly to polenta; or groats, the whole kernel sold roasted as a cereal product.

buk choy also known as bok choy, pak choi, Chinese white cabbage or Chinese chard; has a fresh, mild mustard taste. Use stems and leaves, stir-fried or braised.

butter use salted or unsalted butter; 125g is equal to one stick (4 ounces) of butter.

buttermilk originally the term given to the slightly sour liquid left after butter was churned from cream, today it is made from no-fat or low-fat milk to which specific bacterial cultures have been added. Despite the implication in its name, it is actually low in fat.

cacao

nibs can be separated into cocoa butter and powder. Cocoa powder retains many beneficial antioxidants and is an easy way of adding cocoa into your diet without the kilojoules of chocolate.

raw cacao powder is made by removing the cocoa butter using a process known as cold-pressing. It retains more of its nutrients than heat-processed cacao powder; it also has a stronger, slightly bitter, taste.

capers grey-green buds of a warm climate shrub (usually Mediterranean), sold either dried and salted or pickled in a vinegar brine. Capers must be rinsed well before using.

capsicum (bell pepper) available in red, green, yellow, orange and purplish-black. Discard seeds and membranes before use.

cardamom a spice native to India and used extensively in its cuisine; available in pod, seed or ground form. Has a distinctive aromatic, sweetly rich flavour.

cashews plump, kidney-shaped, golden-brown nuts having a distinctive sweet, buttery flavour and containing about 48% fat.

cavolo nero also called tuscan cabbage; it has long, narrow, wrinkled leaves and a rich and astringent, mild cabbage flavour. It doesn't lose its volume like silver beet or spinach when cooked, but it does need longer cooking.

cheese

blue mould-treated cheeses mottled with blue veining. Varieties include firm and crumbly stilton types and mild, creamy brie-like cheeses.

bocconcini from the diminutive of boccone meaning mouthful, is the term used for walnut-sized, baby mozzarella, a delicate, semi-soft, white cheese traditionally made in Italy from buffalo milk. Spoils rapidly so must be refrigerated, in brine, for 1 or 2 days at most.

cheddar the most common cow's milk 'tasty' cheese; should be aged, hard and have a pronounced bite.

cream commonly called philadelphia or philly; a soft cow-milk cheese, its fat content ranges from 14 to 33%.

fetta Greek in origin; a crumbly textured goat- or sheep-milk cheese with a sharp, salty taste.

goat's made from goat's milk, has an earthy, strong taste; available in both soft and firm textures, in various shapes and sizes, and sometimes rolled in ash or herbs.

gruyère a hard-rind Swiss cheese with small holes and a nutty, slightly salty flavour. A popular cheese for soufflés.

haloumi a Greek Cypriot cheese with a semi-firm, spongy texture and very salty sweet flavour. Ripened and stored in salted whey; best grilled or fried, it holds its shape well on being heated. Eat while still warm as it becomes tough and rubbery on cooling.

mozzarella a soft, spun-curd cheese. It has a low melting point and an elastic texture when heated and is used to add texture rather than flavour.

parmesan also called parmigiano; is a hard, grainy cow-milk cheese originating in Italy.

ricotta a soft, sweet, moist, white cow-milk cheese with a low fat content and a slightly grainy texture. The name roughly translates as 'cooked again' and refers to ricotta's manufacture from a whey that is itself a by-product of other cheese making.

chia seeds contain protein, all the essential amino acids and a wealth of vitamins, minerals and antioxidants, as well as being fibre-rich.

chickpeas (garbanzo beans) also called hummus or channa; an irregularly round, sandy-coloured legume. Available canned or dried (soak in cold water before use).

chilli generally, the smaller the chilli, the hotter it is. Use rubber gloves when seeding and chopping fresh chillies as they can burn your skin. Removing seeds and membranes lessens the heat level.

chives related to the onion and leek; has a subtle onion flavour. Used more for flavour than as an ingredient; chopped finely, they're good in sauces, dressings, omelettes or as a garnish.

chocolate

dark (semi-sweet) made of a high percentage of cocoa liquor and cocoa butter, and little added sugar. It is ideal for desserts and cakes.

white contains no cocoa solids but derives its sweet flavour from cocoa butter. Very sensitive to heat so be careful if melting.

chorizo sausage of Spanish origin, made of coarsely ground pork and highly seasoned with garlic and chilli. They are deeply smoked, very spicy and dry-cured so that they do not need cooking. They are served cold with bread, pickled vegetables and glass of sherry as a tapa (snack), or may be grilled or fried.

cinnamon available in pieces (called sticks or quills) and ground into powder; one of the world's most common spices.

cocoa powder dried, unsweetened, roasted then ground cocoa beans (cacao seeds).

dutch-processed is treated with an alkali to neutralize its acids. It has a reddish-brown colour, mild flavour, and is easy to dissolve in liquids.

coconut

cream comes from the first pressing of the coconut flesh, without the addition of water; the second pressing (less rich) is sold as coconut milk. Look for coconut cream labelled as 100% coconut, without added emulsifiers.

desiccated concentrated, unsweetened, dried and finely shredded coconut flesh.

flaked dried flaked coconut flesh.

flour is a low carbohydrate, high fibre, gluten-free flour made from fresh dried coconut flesh. It has a sweetish taste and is suitable for those on a paleo diet.

milk not the liquid found inside the fruit (coconut water), but the diluted liquid from the second pressing of the white flesh of a mature coconut (the first pressing produces coconut cream).

oil is extracted from the coconut flesh so you don't get any of the fibre, protein or carbohydrates present in the whole coconut. The best quality is virgin coconut oil, which is the oil pressed from the dried coconut flesh, and doesn't include the use of solvents or other refining processes.

shredded thin strips of dried coconut.

sugar is not made from coconuts, but the sap of the blossoms of the coconut palm tree. The refined sap looks a little like raw or light brown sugar, and has a similar caramel flavour. It also has the same amount of kilojoules as regular white (granulated) sugar.

water is the liquid from the centre of a young green coconut. It has fewer kilojoules than fruit juice, with no fat or protein. There are sugars present, but these are slowly absorbed giving coconut water a low GI.

corn, puffed whole grain corn is steamed until it puffs up.

cornflour (cornstarch) thickening agent available in two forms: 100% corn (maize), which is gluten free, and a wheaten cornflour (made from wheat) which is not.

cream

sour a thick commercially-cultured soured cream with a 35% fat content.

thickened (heavy) a whipping cream that contains a thickener; it has a minimum fat content of 35%.

dukkah an Egyptian specialty spice mixture made up of roasted nuts, seeds and an array of aromatic spices.

edamame (shelled soy beans) available frozen from Asian food stores and some supermarkets.

fish sauce also called nam pla or nuoc nam; made from pulverised salted fermented fish, most often anchovies.

flour

brown rice retains the outer bran layer of the rice grain. Contains no gluten. It has a slightly chewy texture and nut-like flavour.

buckwheat not actually a form of wheat, but a herb in the same plant family as rhubarb; it is gluten-free. Has a strong nutty taste.

chickpea (besan) also called gram; made from ground chickpeas so is gluten-free and high in protein.

gluten-free plain (all-purpose) a blend of gluten-free flours and starches (may include corn, potato, tapioca, chickpea and rice).

gluten-free self-raising made similarly to gluten-free plain flour, but with the addition of gluten-free bicarbonate of soda (baking soda).

gluten-free pastry made from a blend of gluten-free flours and starches (may include corn, rice, tapioca, potato starch, pea) and binding and raising agents. Available in health-food stores, and in the health-food section of most supermarkets.

potato made from cooked, dehydrated and ground potato; not to be confused with potato starch which is made from potato starch only. Potato flour has a strong potato flavour and is a heavy flour so a little goes a long way.

rice very fine, almost powdery, gluten-free flour; made from ground white rice.

garam masala a blend of spices that includes cardamom, cinnamon, coriander, cloves, fennel and cumin.

ghee a type of clarified butter used in Indian cooking; milk solids are cooked until golden brown, which imparts a nutty flavour and sweet aroma; it can be heated to a high temperature without burning.

ginger

fresh also called green or root ginger; thick gnarled root of a tropical plant.

glacé fresh ginger root preserved in sugar syrup; crystallised ginger (sweetened with cane sugar) can be substituted if rinsed with warm water and dried before using.

ground also called powdered ginger; used as a flavouring in baking but cannot be substituted for fresh ginger.

pickled pink or red in colour, paper-thin shavings of ginger pickled in a mixture of vinegar, sugar and natural colouring.

goji berries (dried) small, very juicy, sweet red berries that grow on a type of shrub in Tibet. Believed to be high in nutrients and antioxidants.

golden syrup a by-product of refined sugarcane; pure maple syrup or honey can be substituted.

honey the variety sold in a squeezable container is not suitable for the recipes in this book.

kaffir lime leaves sold fresh, dried or frozen; looks like two glossy dark green leaves joined end to end, forming an hourglass shape. Dried leaves are less potent, so double the number called for in a recipe if you substitute them for fresh. A strip of lime peel may be substituted for each leaf.

lemon curd, gluten-free a smooth spread, usually made from lemons, butter and eggs.

lentils (red, brown, yellow) dried pulses often identified by and named after their colour.

French-style green lentils related to the famous French lentils du puy; these green-blue, tiny lentils have a nutty, earthy flavour and a hardy nature that allows them to be rapidly cooked without disintegrating.

macadamias native to Australia; fairly large, slightly soft, buttery rich nut. Used to make oil and macadamia butter; equally good in salads or cakes and pastries; delicious eaten on their own.

maple syrup, pure a thin syrup distilled from the sap of the maple tree. Maple-flavoured syrup or pancake syrup is not an adequate substitute for the real thing.

miso fermented soybean paste. There are many types of miso, each with its own aroma, flavour, colour and texture; it can be kept, airtight, for up to a year in the fridge.

mixed baby leaves also called salad mix or mesclun; a mixture of assorted young lettuce and other green leaves.

mixed spice a blend of ground spices usually cinnamon, allspice and nutmeg.

mushrooms

button small, cultivated white mushrooms with a mild flavour.

dried porcini also known as cèpes; the richest-flavoured mushrooms. Expensive, but because they're so strongly flavoured, only a small amount is required.

flat large, flat mushrooms with a rich earthy flavour, ideal for filling and barbecuing. Are sometimes misnamed field mushrooms, which are wild mushrooms.

shiitake, fresh also known as chinese black, forest or golden oak mushrooms; although cultivated, they are large and meaty and have the earthiness and taste of wild mushrooms.

swiss brown also called roman or cremini. Light to dark brown mushrooms with full-bodied flavour; suited for use in casseroles or being stuffed and baked.

noodles, dried rice also known as rice stick noodles. Made from rice flour and water, available flat and wide or very thin (vermicelli). Must be soaked in boiling water to soften.

oil

coconut see *coconut*

cooking spray we use a cholesterol-free cooking spray made from canola oil, unless stated otherwise.

macadamia oil see *macadamias*

olive made from ripened olives. Extra virgin and virgin are the best, while extra light or light refers to taste not fat levels.

sesame used as a flavouring rather than a cooking medium.

onions

brown and white are interchangeable; white onions have a more pungent flesh.

green (scallions) also called, incorrectly, shallot; an immature onion picked before the bulb has formed, has a long, bright-green stalk.

red also known as spanish, red spanish or bermuda onion; a sweet-flavoured, large, purple-red onion.

shallots also called french or golden shallots or eschalots; small and brown-skinned.

orange blossom water concentrated flavouring made from orange blossoms.

paprika ground, dried, sweet red capsicum (bell pepper); there are many grades and types available, including sweet, hot, mild and smoked.

pancetta an Italian unsmoked bacon, pork belly cured in salt and spices then rolled into a sausage shape and dried for several weeks.

passata sieved tomato puree. To substitute, puree and sieve canned tomatoes or use canned tomato puree which is similar, but slightly thicker.

pecans native to the US and now grown locally; pecans are golden brown, buttery and rich.

pepitas (pumpkin seed kernals) are the pale green kernels of dried pumpkin seeds.

pine nuts not a nut but a small, cream-coloured kernel from pine cones. Toast before use to bring out their flavour.

pistachios green, delicately flavoured nuts inside hard off-white shells. Available salted or unsalted in their shells; you can also get them shelled.

polenta also called cornmeal; a flourlike cereal made of dried corn (maize) sold ground in different textures.

pomegranate dark-red, leathery-skinned fruit about the size of an orange filled with hundreds of seeds, each wrapped in an edible lucent-crimson pulp with a unique tangy sweet-sour flavour.

pomegranate molasses not to be confused with pomegranate syrup or grenadine which is used in cocktails; pomegranate molasses is thicker, browner and more concentrated in flavour, tart and sharp, slightly sweet and fruity. Buy from Middle Eastern food stores or specialty food shops.

preserved lemon rind a North African specialty; lemons are quartered and preserved in salt and lemon juice or water. To use, remove and discard pulp, squeeze juice from rind, rinse rind well; slice thinly. Once opened, store under refrigeration.

quinoa pronounced keen-wa; is the seed of a leafy plant similar to spinach. It has a delicate, slightly nutty taste and chewy texture.

flakes the grains have been rolled and flattened.

puffed has been steamed until it puffs up.

raisins dried sweet grapes.

rhubarb has thick, celery-like stalks; the stalks are the only edible portion of the plant – the leaves contain a toxic substance. Though rhubarb is generally eaten as a fruit, it is a vegetable.

rice

brown retains the high-fibre, nutritious bran coating that's removed from white rice when hulled. It takes longer to cook than white rice and has a chewier texture. Once cooked, the long grains stay separate, while the short grains are soft and stickier.

jasmine or Thai jasmine, is a long-grained white rice recognised around the world as having a perfumed aromatic quality; moist in texture, it clings together after cooking. Sometimes substituted for basmati rice.

rice cereal, gluten-free baby made from ground rice and sunflower oil; always check the packaging as some may also contain traces of wheat, milk and soy.

sugar

brown a very soft, fine granulated sugar retaining molasses for its characteristic colour and flavour.

caster (superfine) finely granulated table sugar.

gluten-free icing (confectioners') also called powdered sugar; pulverised granulated sugar crushed together with a small amount of corn (maize) cornflour (cornstarch).

sumac a purple-red, astringent spice ground from berries growing on shrubs flourishing wild around the Mediterranean; adds a tart, lemony flavour to food. Available from major supermarkets.

tahini is a sesame seed paste available from Middle-Eastern food stores and some supermarkets.

tamari a thick, dark soy sauce made mainly from soy beans and without the wheat used in standard soy sauce.

tamarind the tamarind tree produces clusters of hairy brown pods, each of which is filled with seeds and a viscous pulp, that are dried and pressed into the blocks of tamarind found in Asian food shops. Gives a sweet-sour, slightly astringent taste to marinades, pastes, sauces and dressings.

tamarind concentrate (or paste) the distillation of tamarind pulp into a condensed, compacted paste. Thick and purple-black, it requires no soaking.

turmeric a member of the ginger family; must be grated or pounded to release its acrid aroma and pungent flavour. Known for the golden colour it imparts, fresh turmeric can be substituted with the more commonly found dried powder.

vanilla

bean dried, long, thin pod from a tropical golden orchid; the minuscule black seeds inside the bean impart a luscious flavour in baking and desserts.

extract made by extracting the flavour from the vanilla bean pod; the pods are soaked, usually in alcohol, to capture the authentic flavour.

paste made from vanilla beans and contains real seeds. Is highly concentrated: 1 teaspoon replaces a whole bean.

xanthan gum is a thickening agent produced by fermentation of, usually, corn sugar. When buying xanthan gum, ensure the packet states 'made from fermented corn sugar'. Found in the health-food section in larger supermarkets.

yeast (dried and fresh), a raising agent used in dough making. Granular (7g sachets) and fresh compressed (20g blocks) yeast can almost always be substituted for the other.

yoghurt, Greek-style plain yoghurt strained in a cloth (traditionally muslin) to remove the whey and to give it a creamy consistency.

zucchini also called courgette.

CONVERSION CHART

MEASURES

One Australian metric measuring cup holds approximately 250ml; one Australian metric tablespoon holds 20ml; one Australian metric teaspoon holds 5ml.

The difference between one country's measuring cups and another's is within a two- or three-teaspoon variance, and will not affect your cooking results.

North America, New Zealand and the United Kingdom use a 15ml tablespoon. All cup and spoon measurements are level. The most accurate way of measuring dry ingredients is to weigh them. When measuring liquids, use a clear glass or plastic jug with the metric markings.

We use large eggs with an average weight of 60g.

DRY MEASURES

metric	imperial
15g	½oz
30g	1oz
60g	2oz
90g	3oz
125g	4oz (¼lb)
155g	5oz
185g	6oz
220g	7oz
250g	8oz (½lb)
280g	9oz
315g	10oz
345g	11oz
375g	12oz (¾lb)
410g	13oz
440g	14oz
470g	15oz
500g	16oz (1lb)
750g	24oz (1½lb)
1kg	32oz (2lb)

LIQUID MEASURES

metric	imperial
30ml	1 fluid oz
60ml	2 fluid oz
100ml	3 fluid oz
125ml	4 fluid oz
150ml	5 fluid oz
190ml	6 fluid oz
250ml	8 fluid oz
300ml	10 fluid oz
500ml	16 fluid oz
600ml	20 fluid oz
1000ml (1 litre)	1¾ pints

LENGTH MEASURES

metric	imperial
3mm	⅛in
6mm	¼in
1cm	½in
2cm	¾in
2.5cm	1in
5cm	2in
6cm	2½in
8cm	3in
10cm	4in
13cm	5in
15cm	6in
18cm	7in
20cm	8in
22cm	9in
25cm	10in
28cm	11in
30cm	12in (1ft)

OVEN TEMPERATURES

The oven temperatures in this book are for conventional ovens; if you have a fan-forced oven, decrease the temperature by 10-20 degrees.

	°C (Celsius)	°F (Fahrenheit)
Very slow	120	250
Slow	150	300
Moderately slow	160	325
Moderate	180	350
Moderately hot	200	400
Hot	220	425
Very hot	240	475

THE IMPERIAL MEASUREMENTS USED IN THESE RECIPES ARE APPROXIMATE ONLY. MEASUREMENTS FOR CAKE PANS ARE APPROXIMATE ONLY. USING SAME-SHAPED CAKE PANS OF A SIMILAR SIZE SHOULD NOT AFFECT THE OUTCOME OF YOUR BAKING. WE MEASURE THE INSIDE TOP OF THE CAKE PAN TO DETERMINE SIZES.

INDEX